Love's Pilgrimage by Francis Beaumont & John Fletcher

The English dramatists Francis Beaumont and John Fletcher, collaborated in their writing during the reign of James I of England (James VI of Scotland, 1567–1625; in England he reigned from 1603).

Beaumont & Fletcher began to collaborate as writers soon after they met. After notable failures of their solo works their first joint effort, Philaster, was a success and tragicomedy was the genre they explored and built upon. There would be many further successes to follow.

There is an account that at the time the two men shared everything. They lived together in a house on the Bankside in Southwark, "they also lived together in Bankside, sharing clothes and having one wench in the house between them." Or as another account puts it "sharing everything in the closest intimacy."

Whatever the truth of this they were now recognised as perhaps the best writing team of their generation, so much so, that their joint names was applied to all the works in which either, or both, had a pen including those with Philip Massinger, James Shirley and Nathan Field.

The first Beaumont and Fletcher folio of 1647 contained 35 plays; 53 plays were included in the second folio in 1679. Other works bring the total plays in the canon to about 55. However there appears here to have been some duplicity on the account of the publishers who seemed to attribute so many to the team. It is now thought that the work between solely by Beaumont and Fletcher amounts to approximately 15 plays, though of course further works by them were re-worked by others and the originals lost.

After Beaumont's early death in 1616 Fletcher continued to write and, at his height was, by many standards, the equal of Shakespeare in popularity until his own death in 1625.

Index of Contents

ACTUS QUINTUS
SCÆNA PRIMA
SCÆNA SECUNDA
SCÆNA TERTIA
SCÆNA QUARTA
SCÆNA QUINTA
FRANCIS BEAUMONT – A SHORT BIOGRAPHY
JOHN FLETCHER – A SHORT BIOGRAPHY
FRANCIS BEAUMONT & JOHN FLETCHER – A CONCISE BIBLIOGRAPHY

DRAMATIS PERSONAE
MEN
Governor of Barcellona.
Leonardo, a noble Genoese, Father to Mark Antonio.
Don Sanchio, an old lame angry Soldier, Father to Leocadia.
Alphonso, a cholerick Don, Father to Theodosia.
Philippo, Son to Alphonso, Lover of Leocadia.
Mark-Antonio, Son to Leonardo.
Pedro, a Gentleman and friend to Leonardo.
Rodorigo, General of the Spanish Gallies.
Incubo, Bailiff of Castel Bianco.
Diego, Host of Ossuna.
Lazaro, Hostler to Diego.
Host of Barcellona.
Bailiff of Barcellona.
Chirurgeons.
Soldiers.
Attendants.
Townsmen.
Attendants.
WOMEN
Theodosia, Daugh. to Alphonso. Leocadia, Daugh. to Don
Sanchio. Love-sick Ladies in pursuit of M. Anton.
Eugenia, Wife to the Governor of Barcellona.
Hostess, Wife to Diego.
Hostess, Wife to the Host of Barcellona.

SCENE: Barcelona and the Road.

PROLOGUE

To this place Gentlemen, full many a day
We have bid ye welcome; and to many a Play:
And those whose angry souls were not diseas'd

With Law, or lending Money, we have pleas'd;
And make no doubt to do again. This night
No mighty matter, nor no light,
We must intreat you look for: A good tale,
Told in two hours, we will not fail
If we be perfect, to rehearse ye: New
I am sure it is, and handsome; but how true
Let them dispute that writ it. Ten to one
We please the Women, and I would know that man
Follows not their example? If ye mean
To know the Play well, travel with the Scene.
For it lies upon the Road; if we chance tire,
As ye are good men, leave us not i'th' mire,
Another bait may mend us: If you grow
A little gall'd or weary; cry but hoa,
And we'll stay for ye. When our journey ends
Every mans Pot I hope, and all part friends.

ACTUS PRIMUS

SCÆNA PRIMA

Enter **INCUBO** the Bailiff, **DIEGO** the Host.

INCUBO
Signior Don Diego, and mine Host, save thee.

DIEGO
I thank you Mr. Baily.

INCUBO
O the block!

DIEGO
Why, how should I have answer'd?

INCUBO
Not with that
Negligent rudeness: But I kiss your hands
Signior Don Incubo de Hambre, and then
My Titles: Master Baily of Castle-blanco:
Thou ne'r wilt have the elegancy of an Host;
I sorrow for thee, as my friend and Gossip:
No smoak, nor steam out-breathing from the kitchen?
There's little life i'th Hearth then.

DIEGO
I, there, there,
That is his friendship, harkening for the spit,
And sorrow that he cannot smell the pot boil.

INCUBO
Strange
An Inn should be so curst, and not the sign
Blasted, nor withered; very strange, three days now,
And not an Egg eat in it, nor an Onion.

DIEGO
I think they ha' strew'd the high-ways with caltraps, I,
No horse dares pass 'em; I did never know
A week of so sad doings, since I first
Stood to my Sign-post.

INCUBO
Gossip, I have found
The root of all: kneel, pray, it is thy self
Art cause thereof: each person is the Founder
Of his own fortune, good or bad; but mend it,
Call for thy Cloak, and Rapier.

DIEGO
How?

INCUBO
Do, call,
And put 'em on in haste: Alter thy fortune,
By appearing worthy of her: Dost thou think
Her good face e'r will know a man in cuerpo?
In single body, thus? in Hose, and Doublet
The horse-boys garb? base blank, and halfe blank cuerpo?
Did I, or Mr Dean of Sivil our neighbor
E'r reach our dignities in cuerpo, think'st thou,
In squirting Hose and Doublet? Signior, no,
There went more to't: there were Cloaks, Gowns, Cassocks,
And other paramentos; Call, I say,
His Cloak, and Rapier here.

[Enter **HOSTESS**.

HOSTESS
What means your Worship?

INCUBO
Bring forth thy Husbands Sword: so hang it on,

[**HOSTESS** brings in sword and then cloak.

And now his cloak, here cast it up; I mean
Gossip, to change your luck, and bring you guests.

HOSTESS
Why? is there charm in this?

INCUBO
Expect; now walk,
But not the pace of one that runs on errands;
For, want of gravity in an Host, is odious:
You may remember Gossip, if you please,
(Your Wife being then th' Infanta of the Gipsies,
And your self governing a great mans Mules then)
Me a poor Squire at Madrid attending
A Master of Ceremonies; But a man, believe it,
That knew his place to the gold weight, and such
Have I heard him oft say, ought every Host
Within the Catholique Kings Dominions
Be in his own house.

DIEGO
How?

INCUBO
A Master of Ceremonies;
At least Vice-Master, and to do nought in cuerpo,
That was his Maxim, I will tell thee of him:
He would not speak with an Ambassadors Cook,
See a cold bake-meat from a forreign part
In cuerpo: had a dog but staid without,
Or beast of quality, as an English Cow,
But to present it self, he would put on
His Savoy chain about his neck, the ruff
And cuffs of Holland, then the Naples Hat
With the Rome Hat-band, and the Florentine Agat,
The Millan Sword, the Cloak of Genoa, set
With Flemish buttons; all his given pieces
To entertain 'em in, and complement
With a tame Conie, as with the Prince that sent it.

[Knock within.

DIEGO
List. Who is there?

INCUBO
A guest and 't be thy will.

DIEGO
Look Spowse, cry luck, and we be encounter'd: ha?

HOSTESS
Luck then, and good, for 'tis a fine brave guest,
With a brave horse.

INCUBO
Why now, believe of cuerpo.

[Enter **THEODOSIA**.

As you shall see occasion: go, and meet him.

THEODOSIA
Look to my horse, I pray you, well.

DIEGO
He shall, Sir.

INCUBO
Oh how beneath his rank and call was that now?
Your horse shall be entreated as becomes
A horse of fashion, and his inches.

THEODOSIA
Oh.

[Faints.

INCUBO
Look to the Cavalier: what ails he? stay
If it concern his horse, let it not trouble him,
He shall have all respect the place can yield him
Either of barley, or fresh straw.

DIEGO
Good Sir
Look up.

INCUBO
He sinks, somewhat to cast upon him,
He'll go away in cuerpo else.

DIEGO

What, Wife!
Oh your hot waters quickly, and some cold
To cast in his sweet face.

HOSTESS
Alas, fair flower?

[Exit.

DIEGO
Does any body entertain his Horse?

HOSTESS
Yes, Lazaro has him.

[Enter **HOSTESS** with a glass of water.

INCUBO
Go you see him in person.

[Exit **DIEGO**.

HOSTESS
Sir, taste a little of this, of mine own water,
I did distill't my self; sweet Lilly look upon me,
You are but newly blown, my pretty Tulip.
Faint not upon your stalk, 'tis firm and fresh
Stand up so bolt upright, you are yet in growing.

THEODOSIA
Pray you let me have a chamber.

HOSTESS
That you shall, Sir.

THEODOSIA
And where I may be private, I intreat you.

HOSTESS
For that in troth Sir, we ha no choice: our house
Is but a vent of need, that now and then
Receives a guest, between the greater Towns
As they come late; only one room.

INCUBO
She means, Sir, it is none
Of those wild, scatter'd heaps, call'd Inns, where scarce
The Host is heard, though he wind his horn t' his people,

Here is a competent pile, wherein the man,
Wife, Servants, all do live within the whistle.

HOSTESS
Only one room.

INCUBO
A pretty modest quadrangle
She will describe to you.

HOSTESS
Wherein stands two Beds Sir.

[Enter **DIEGO**.

We have, and where, if any guest do come,
He must of force be lodg'd, that is the truth, Sir.

THEODOSIA
But if I pay you for both your beds, methinks
That should alike content you.

HOSTESS
That it shall, Sir.
If I be paid, I am paid.

THEODOSIA
Why, there's a Ducat

[Giving money.

Will that make your content?

HOSTESS
Oh the sweet face on you:
A Ducket? yes, and there were three beds Sir,
And twice so many rooms, which is one more,
You should be private in 'em all, in all Sir,
No one should have a piece of a bed with you
Not master Dean of Sivil himself, I swear.
Though he came naked hither, as once he did
When h' had like t'have been tane a bed with the Moor
And guelt by her Master: you shall be as private,
As if you lay in's own great house that's haunted,
Where no body comes, they say.

THEODOSIA
I thank you Hostess.

Pray you, will you shew me in.

HOSTESS
Yes marry will I Sir,
And pray that not a flea, or a chink vex you.

[Exit **HOSTESS** and **THEODOSIA**.

INCUBO
You forget supper: Gossip: move for supper.

DIEGO
'Tis strange what love to a beast may do, his Horse
Threw him into this fit.

INCUBO
You shall excuse me
It was his being in cuerpo, meerly caus'd it.

DIEGO
Do you think so Sir?

INCUBO
Most unlucky cuerpo.
Naught else, he looks as he would eat Partridge,
This guest; ha' you 'em ready in the house?
And a fine piece of Kid now? and fresh garlick

[Enter **HOSTESS**.

With Sardinia and Zant Oil? how now?
Has he bespoke, what will he have a brace,
Or but one Partridge, or a short leg'd Hen,
Daintyly carbonado'd?

HOSTESS
'Lass the dead
May be as ready for a supper as he.

INCUBO
Ha?

HOSTESS
He has no mind to eat, more than his shadow.

INCUBO
Say you.

DIEGO

How does your worship?

INCUBO

I put on
My left shooe first to day, now I perceive it,
And skipt a bead in saying 'em 'ore; else
I could not be thus cross'd: He cannot be
Above seventeen; one of his years, and have
No better a stomach?

HOSTESS

And in such good cloaths too.

DIEGO

Nay, these do often make the stomach worse, wife,
That is no reason.

INCUBO

I could, at his years, Gossips
(As temperate as you see me now) have eaten
My brace of Ducks, with my half Goose, my Conie,
And drink my whole twelve Marvedis in Wine
As easie as I now get down three Olives.

DIEGO

And, with your temperance-favour, yet I think
Your worship would put to't at six and thirty
For a good wager; and the meal in too.

INCUBO

I do not know what mine old mouth can do.
I ha not prov'd it lately.

DIEGO

That's the grief, Sir.

INCUBO

But is he without hope then gone to bed?

HOSTESS

I fear so, Sir, h'as lock'd the door close to him
Sure he is very ill.

INCUBO

That is with fasting,
You should ha told him Gossip, what you had had,
Given him the Inventory of your kitchen,

It is the picklock in an Inn, and often
Opens a close barr'd stomach: what may he be troh?
Has he so good a Horse?

DIEGO
Oh a brave Jennet,
As e'r your worship saw.

INCUBO
And he eats?

DIEGO
Strongly.

INCUBO
A mighty Solecisme, heaven give me patience,
What creatures has he?

HOSTESS
None.

INCUBO
And so well cloath'd,
And so well mounted?

DIEGO
That's all my wonder, Sir,
Who he should be; he is attir'd and hors'd
For the Constables Son of Spain.

INCUBO
My wonders more
He should want appetite: well a good night
To both my Gossips: I will for this time
Put off the thought of supping: In the morning
Remember him of breakfast pray you.

HOSTESS
I shall Sir.

DIEGO
A hungry time Sir.

INCUBO
We that live like mice
On others meat, must watch when we can get it.

[Exit **INCUBO**.

HOSTESS
Yes, but I would not tell him: Our fair guest
Says, though he eats no supper he will pay for one.

DIEGO
Good news: we'll eat it spouse, t' his health,
'Twas politickly done t'admit no sharers.

[Enter **PHILIPPO**.

PHILIPPO
Look to the Mules there, where's mine Host?

DIEGO
Here Sir.
Another Fayerie.

HOSTESS
Bless me.

PHILIPPO
From what sweet Hostess?
Are you afraid o' your guests?

HOSTESS
From Angels, Sir,
I think there's none but such come here to night,
My house had never so good luck afore
For brave, fine guests; and yet the ill luck on't is
I cannot bid you welcome.

PHILIPPO
No?

HOSTESS
Not lodge you Sir.

PHILIPPO
Not, Hostess?

HOSTESS
No in troth Sir, I do tell you
Because you may provide in time: my beds
Are both tane up by a young Cavalier
That will and must be private.

DIEGO

He has paid Sir
For all our Chambers.

HOSTESS
Which is one: and Beds
Which I already ha told you are two: But Sir,
So sweet a creature, I am very sorry
I cannot lodge you by him; you look so like him
Yo' are both the loveliest pieces.

PHILIPPO
What train has he?

DIEGO
None but himself.

PHILIPPO
And will no less than both beds
Serve him?

HOSTESS
H'as given me a Ducat for 'em.

PHILIPPO
Oh.
You give me reason Hostess: Is he handsome,
And young do you say?

HOSTESS
Oh Sir, the delicat'st flesh
And finest cloths withal, and such a horse,
With such a Saddle.

PHILIPPO
She's in love with all.
The horse and him, and Saddle, and cloths, good woman,
Thou justifiest thy Sex; lov'st all that's brave:

[Enter **INCUBO**.

Sure though I lye o'th' ground, I'll stay here now
And have a sight of him: you'll give me house-room,
Fire, and fresh meat, for money, gentle Hostess;
And make me a pallat?

INCUBO
Sir, she shall do reason....
I understood you had another Guest, Gossips,

Pray you let his Mule be lookt to, have good straw,
And store of bran: And Gossip, do you hear,
Let him not stay for supper: What good Fowl ha' you?
This Gentleman would eat a Pheasant.

HOSTESS
'Lass Sir;
We ha' no such.

INCUBO
I kiss your hands fair Sir.
What ha you then? speak what you have? I'm one Sir
Here for the Catholique King, an Officer
T' enquire what guests come to these places; you Sir
Appear a person of quality, and 'tis fit
You be accommodated: why speak you not,
What ha' you Woman? are you afraid to vent
That which you have?

PHILIPPO
This is a most strange man;
T' appoint my meat.

HOSTESS
The half of a cold hen, Sir,
And a boil'd quarter of Kid, is all i'th' house.

INCUBO
Why all's but cold; let him see it forth,
Cover, and give the eye some satisfaction,
A Travellers stomach must see bread and salt,
His belly is nearer to him, than his kindred;
Cold hen's a pretty meat Sir.

PHILIPPO
What you please;
I am resolv'd t' obey.

INCUBO
So is your Kid,
With Pepper, Garlick, and the juyce of an Orange:
She shall with Sallads help it, and clean linnen;
Dispatch;

[Exeunt **HOSTESS** and **DIEGO**.

What news at Court Sir?

PHILIPPO
Faith, new tires
Most of the Ladies have, the men old Suits:
Only the Kings Fool has a new Coat
To serve you.

INCUBO
I did guess you came from thence, Sir.

PHILIPPO
But I do know I did not.

INCUBO
I mistook Sir.
What hear you of the Archdukes?

PHILIPPO
Troth your question.

[Enter **HOSTESS** and **SERVANTS** with Table.

INCUBO
Of the French business, What?

PHILIPPO
As much.

INCUBO
No more?
They say the French: Oh that's well: come, I'll help you:
Have you no Jiblets now? or a broil'd rasher.
Or some such present dish t' assist?

HOSTESS
Not any Sir.

INCUBO
The more your fault: you nev'r should be without
Such aids: what cottage would ha' lack'd a Pheasant
At such a time as this? well, bring your Hen,
And Kid forth quickly.

PHILIPPO
That should be my prayer
To scape his Inquisition.

INCUBO
Sir, the French,

They say are divided 'bout their match with us,
What think you of it.

PHILIPPO
As of naught to me, Sir.

INCUBO
Nay, it's as little to me too: but I love
To ask after these things, to know the affections
Of States and Princes, now and then for bettring.

PHILIPPO
Of your own ignorance.

INCUBO
Yes Sir:

PHILIPPO
Many do so.

INCUBO
I cannot live without it: what do you hear
Of our Indian Fleet; they say they are well return'd.

PHILIPPO
I had no venture with 'em Sir; had you?

[Enter **HOSTESS** and **SERVANTS** with meat.

INCUBO
Why do you ask Sir?

PHILIPPO
'Cause it might concern you,
It does not me.

INCUBO
Oh here's your meat come.

PHILIPPO
Thanks,
I welcome it at any price.

INCUBO
Some stools here,
And bid mine Host bring Wine, I'll try your Kid,
If he be sweet: he looks well.

[Tastes it.

Yes, he is good;
I'll carve you Sir.

PHILIPPO
You use me too too Princely:
Tast, and carve too.

INCUBO
I love to do these Offices.

PHILIPPO
I think you do: for whose sake?

INCUBO
For themselves Sir,
The very doing of them is reward.

PHILIPPO
'Had little faith would not believe you, Sir.

INCUBO
Gossip, some Wine.

*[Enter **DIEGO** with Wine.*

DIEGO
Here 'tis: and right St. Martyn.

INCUBO
Measure me out a glass.

PHILIPPO
I love the humanity
Us'd in this place:

INCUBO
Sir, I salute you here.

[Drinks.

PHILIPPO
I kiss your hands Sir.

INCUBO
Good wine, it will beget an appetite:
Fill him, and sit down, Gossip, entertain

Your noble guest here, as becomes your title.

DIEGO
Please you to like this Wine Sir?

PHILIPPO
I dislike
Nothing mine Host, but that I may not see
Your conceal'd guest: here's to you.

DIEGO
In good faith Sir;
I wish you as well as him: would you might see him

INCUBO
And wherefore may he not:

DIEGO
'Has lock'd himself Sir
Up, and has hir'd both the beds o' my wife
At extraordinary rate.

PHILIPPO
I'll give as much
If that will do't, for one, as he for both;
What say you mine Host, the door once open
I'll fling my self upon the next bed to him
And there's an end of me till morning; noise
I will make none

DIEGO
I wish your worship well—but—

INCUBO
His honor is engag'd: And my she-Gossip
Hath past her promise, hath she not?

DIEGO
Yes truly:

INCUBO
That toucheth to the credit of the house:
Well, I will eat a little, and think: how say you Sir
Unto this brawn o'th' Hen?

PHILIPPO
I ha' more mind
To get this bed Sir.

INCUBO

Say you so: Why then
Giv't me agen, and drink to me: mine Host
Fill him his Wine: thou'rt dull, and dost not praise it,
I eat but to teach you the way Sir.

PHILIPPO

Sir:
Find but the way to lodge me in this chamber
I'll give mine Host two Duckets for his bed,
And you Sir two Reals: here's to you—

[Drinks.

INCUBO

Excuse me,
I am not mercenary: Gossip pledge him for me,
I'll think a little more; but ev'n one bit
And then talk on: you cannot interrupt me.

DIEGO

This piece of wine Sir, cost me—

INCUBO

Stay: I have found:
This little morsel, and then: here's excellent garlick:
Have you not a bunch of grapes now: or some Bacon
To give the mouth a relish?

DIEGO

Wife, do you hear?

INCUBO

It is no matter: Sir give mine Host your Ducats.

DIEGO

How Sir?

INCUBO

Do you receive 'em: I will save
The honesty of your house: and yours too Gossip,
And I will lodge the Gentleman: shew the chamber.

DIEGO

Good Sir do you hear.

INCUBO

Shew me the chamber.

DIEGO
Pray you Sir,
Do not disturb my guests.

INCUBO
Disturb? I hope
The Catholick King Sir, may command a lodging
Without disturbing in his Vassals house,
For any Minister of his, emploid
In business of the State. Where is the door?
Open the door, who are you there? within?

[Knocks.

In the Kings name.

[**THEODOSIA** within.

THEODOSIA
What would you have?

INCUBO
Your key Sir,
And your door open: I have here command
To lodge a Gentleman, from the Justice, sent
Upon the Kings affairs.

THEODOSIA
Kings and necessities
Must be obey'd: the key is under the door.

INCUBO
How now Sir, are you fitted? you secur'd?

PHILIPPO
Your two Reals are grown a piece of Eight.

INCUBO
Excuse me Sir.

PHILIPPO
'Twill buy a Hen; and Wine

[Giving money.

Sir, for to morrow.

[Exit **PHILIPPO**.

INCUBO
I do kiss your hands Sir.
Well this will bear my charge yet to the Gallies
Where I am owing a Ducket: whither this night
By the Moons leave I'll march: for in the morning
Early, they put from Port St. Maries. Ex. all but Diego.

[Exeunt all except **DIEGO**.

DIEGO
Lazaro.

[Enter **LAZARO**.

How do the horses?

LAZARO
Would you would go and see Sir,
A — of all Jades, what a clap h'as given me:
As sure as you live Master he knew perfectly
I couzen'd him on's Oats: he lookt upon me
And then he sneer'd, as who should say, take heed sirrah:
And when he saw our half Peck, which you know
Was but an old Court dish, lord how he stampt:
I thought 't had been for joy, when suddenly
He cuts me a back caper with his heels
And takes me just o'th crupper, down came I,
And all my ounce of Oats: Then he neigh'd out
As though he had had a mare by th' tail.

DIEGO
Faith Lazaro
We are to blame to use the poor dumb serviters
So cruelly.

LAZARO
Yonder's this other Gentleman's horse
Keeping our Lady Eve: the devil a bit
H'as got since he came in yet: there he stands
And looks, and looks, but 'tis your pleasure, Sir,
He shall look lean enough: h'as Hay before him
But 'tis as big as Hemp, and will as soon choak him,
Unless he eat it butter'd: he had four shooes
And good ones when he came: 'tis a strange wonder
With standing still he should cast three.

DIEGO

O Lazaro.
The Devil's in this Trade: truth never knew it
And to the devil we shall travel, Lazaro
Unless we mend our manners: once every week
I meet with such a knock to mollifie me
Sometimes a dozen to awake my conscience
Yet still I sleep securely.

LAZARO

Certain Master
We must use better dealing.

DIEGO

'Faith for mine own part
Not to give ill example to our issues,
I could be well content to steal but two girths,
And now and then a saddle-cloth: change a bridle
Only for exercise.

LAZARO

If we could stay there
There were some hope on's Master: but the devil is
We are drunk so early we mistake whole Saddles
Sometimes a horse; and then it seems to us too
Every poor jade has his whole peck, and tumbles
Up to his ears in clean straw, and every bottle
Shews at the least a dozen; when the truth is, Sir,
There's no such matter, not a smell of Provinder,
Not so much straw as would tie up a horse tail,
Nor any thing i'th' rack, but two old Cobwebs
And so much rotten Hay as had been a hens nest.

DIEGO

Well, these mistakings must be mended, Lazaro,
These apparitions, that abuse our sences,
And make us ever apt to sweep the manger
But put in nothing; these fancies must be forgot
And we must pray it may be reveal'd to us
Whose horse we ought, in conscience, to couzen,
And how, and when; A Parsons Horse may suffer
A little greazing in his teeth, 'tis wholsome;
And keeps him in a sober shuffle: and his Saddle
May want a stirrop, and it may be sworn
His Learning lay on one side, and so broke it:
H'as ever Oats in's Cloak-bag to prevent us
And therefore 'tis a meritorious office

To tythe him soundly.

LAZARO
And a Grazier may
(For those are pinching puckfoysts, and suspitious)
Suffer a myst before his eyes sometimes too,
And think he sees his horse eat halfe a bushel:
When the truth is, rubbing his gums with salt,
Till all the skin come off: he shall but mumble
Like an old Woman that were chewing Brawn,
And drop 'em out again.

DIEGO
That may do well too,
And no doubt 'tis but venial, But good Lazaro
Have you a care of understanding horses,
Horses with angry heels, gentlemens horses,
Horses that know the world: let them have meat
Till their teeth ake; and rubbing till their ribs
Shine like a wenches forehead; they are devils.

LAZARO
And look into our dealings: as sure as we live
These Courtiers horses are a kind of Welsh Prophets,
Nothing can be hid from 'em: For mine own part
The next I cozen of that kind shall be founder'd,
And of all four too: I'll no more such complements
Upon my crupper.

DIEGO
Steal but a little longer
Till I am lam'd too, and we'll repent together,
It will not be above two daies.

LAZARO
By that time
I shall be well again, and all forgot Sir.

DIEGO
Why then I'll stay for thee.

[Exit.

SCÆNA SECUNDA

Enter **THEODOSIA** and **PHILIPPO** on several Beds.

THEODOSIA
Oh,—ho! oh—ho!

PHILIPPO
Ha?

THEODOSIA
Oh—oh! heart—heart—heart—heart?

PHILIPPO
What's that?

THEODOSIA
When wilt thou break?—break, break, break?

PHILIPPO
Ha?
I would the voice were strong, or I nearer.

THEODOSIA
Shame, shame, eternal shame? what have I done?

PHILIPPO
Done?

THEODOSIA
And to no end, what a wild journey
Have I more wildly undertaken?

PHILIPPO
Journey?

THEODOSIA
How, without counsel? care? reason, or fear?

PHILIPPO
Whither will this fit carry?

THEODOSIA
Oh my folly!

PHILIPPO
This is no common sickness.

THEODOSIA
How have I left
All I should love, or keep? oh heaven.

PHILIPPO
Sir?

THEODOSIA
Ha?

PHILIPPO
How do you gentle Sir?

THEODOSIA
Alas my fortune!

PHILIPPO
It seems your sorrow oppresses: please your goodness,
Let me bear half, Sir: a divided burthen
Is so made lighter.

THEODOSIA
Oh!

PHILIPPO
That sigh betraies
The fulness of your grief.

THEODOSIA
I, if that grief
Had not bereft me of my understanding,
I should have well remembred where I was,
And in what company; and clapt a lock
Upon this tongue for talking.

PHILIPPO
Worthy Sir
Let it not add to your grief, that I have heard
A sigh or groan come from you: That is all Sir:

THEODOSIA
Good Sir no more: you have heard too much I fear,
Would I had taken Poppy when I spake it.

PHILIPPO
It seems you have an ill belief of me
And would have fear'd much more, had you spoke ought
I could interpret. But believe it Sir
Had I had means to look into your breast,
And tane you sleeping here, that so securely
I might have read all that your woe would hide

I would not have betraid you.

THEODOSIA
Sir, that speech
Is very noble, and almost would tempt
My need to trust you.

PHILIPPO
At your own election,
I dare not make my faith so much suspected
As to protest again: nor am I curious
To know more than is fit.

THEODOSIA
Sir, I will trust you
But you shall promise Sir to keep your bed,
And whatsoe'r you hear, not to importune
More I beseech you from me.

PHILIPPO
Sir I will not.

THEODOSIA
Than I am prone to utter.

PHILIPPO
My faith for it.

THEODOSIA
If I were wise, I yet should hold my peace.
You will be noble?

PHILIPPO
You shall make me so
If you'll but think me such.

THEODOSIA
I do: then know
You are deceiv'd with whom you have talk'd so long.
I am a most unfortunate lost woman.

PHILIPPO
Ha?

THEODOSIA
Do not stir Sir: I have here a Sword.

PHILIPPO

Not I sweet Lady: of what blood, or name.

THEODOSIA
You'll keep your faith.

PHILIPPO
I'll perish else.

THEODOSIA
Believe then
Of birth too noble for me, so descended—
I am asham'd, no less than I am affrighted.

PHILIPPO
Fear not: by all good things, I will not wrong you.

THEODOSIA
I am the Daughter of a noble Gentleman
Born in this part of Spain: my fathers name Sir:
But why should I abuse that reverence
When a childs duty has forsaken me.

PHILIPPO
All may be mended, in fit time too: speak it.

THEODOSIA
Alphonso, sir.

PHILIPPO
Alphonso? What's your own name?

THEODOSIA
Any base thing you can invent.

PHILIPPO
Deal truly.

THEODOSIA
They call me Theodosia.

PHILIPPO
Ha? and love
Is that that hath chang'd you thus?

THEODOSIA
Ye have observ'd me
Too nearly Sir, 'tis that indeed: 'tis love Sir:
And love of him (oh heavens) why should men deal thus?

Why should they use their arts to cozen us?
That have no cunning, but our fears about us?
And ever that too late too; no dissembling
Or double way but doating: too much loving?
Why should they find new oaths, to make more wretches?

PHILIPPO
What may his name be?

THEODOSIA
Sir, a name that promises
Methinks no such ill usage: Mark-Antonio
A noble neighbors son: Now I must desire ye
To stay a while: else my weak eyes must answer.

PHILIPPO
I will:—Are ye yet ready? what is his quality?

THEODOSIA
His best a thief Sir: that he would be known by
Is heir to Leonardo, a rich Gentleman:
Next of a handsome body, had heaven made him
A mind fit to it. To this man my fortune,
(My more than purblind fortune) gave my faith,
Drawn to it by as many shews of service
And signs of truth, as ever false tongue utter'd:
Heaven pardon all.

PHILIPPO
'Tis well said: forward Lady.

THEODOSIA
Contracted Sir, and by exchange of rings
Our souls deliver'd: nothing left unfinish'd
But the last work, enjoying me, and Ceremony.
For that I must confess was the first wise doubt
I ever made: yet after all this love Sir,
All this profession of his faith; when daily
And hourly I expected the blest Priest
He left me like a dream, as all this story
Had never been, nor thought of, why, I know not;
Yet I have called my conscience to confession,
And every syllable that might offend
I have had in shrift: yet neither loves Law Signior,
Nor tye of Maidens duty, but desiring
Have I transgrest in: left his father too,
Nor whither he is gone, or why departed
Can any tongue resolve me: All my hope

(Which keeps me yet alive, and would perswade me
I may be once more happy, and thus shapes me
A shame to all my modest Sex) is this Sir,
I have a Brother and his old Companion,
Student in Salamanca, there my last hope
If he be yet alive, and can be loving
Is left me to recover him: For which travel
In this Sute left at home of that dear Brothers
Thus as you find me, without fear, or wisdom,
I have wander'd from my Father, fled my friends,
And now am only child of hope and danger:
You are now silent Sir: this tedious story
(That ever keeps me waking) makes you heavy:
'Tis fit it should do so: for that, and I
Can be but troubles.

PHILIPPO
No, I sleep not Lady:
I would I could: oh heaven is this my comfort?

THEODOSIA
What ail you gentle Sir?

PHILIPPO
Oh.

THEODOSIA
Why do you groan so?

PHILIPPO
I must, I must; oh misery;

THEODOSIA
But now Sir,
You were my comfort: if any thing afflict ye
Am not I fit to bear a part on't? and by your own rule?

PHILIPPO
No; if you could heal, as you have wounded me,
But 'tis not in your power.

[Rises.

THEODOSIA
I fear intemperance.

PHILIPPO
Nay, do not seek to shun me: I must see you:

By heaven I must: hoa, there mine Host: a Candle:
Strive not, I will not stir ye.

THEODOSIA
Noble Sir
This is a breach of promise.

PHILIPPO
Tender Lady
It shall be none but necessary: hoa, there,
Some light, some light for heavens sake.

THEODOSIA
Will ye betray me?
Are ye a Gentleman?

PHILIPPO
Good woman:

THEODOSIA
Sir.

[Enter **DIEGO** with a light.

PHILIPPO
If I be prejudicial to you, curse me.

DIEGO
Ye are early stirring Sir.

PHILIPPO
Give me your Candle
And so good morrow for a while.

DIEGO
Good morrow Sir.

[Exit.

THEODOSIA
My Brother Don Philippo: nay Sir, kill me!

[Kneels.

I ask no mercy Sir, for none dare know me,
I can deserve none: As ye look upon me
Behold in infinite these foul dishonors,
My noble Father, then your self, last all

That bear the name of kindred, suffer in me:
I have forgot whose child I am; whose Sister:
Do you forget the pity tied to that:
Let not compassion sway you: you will be then
As foul as I, and bear the same brand with me,
A favourer of my fault: ye have a sword Sir,
And such a cause to kill me in.

PHILIPPO
Rise Sister,

[She rises.

I wear no sword for Women: nor no anger
While your fair chastity is yet untouch'd.

THEODOSIA
By those bright Stars, it is Sir.

PHILIPPO
For my Sister
I do believe ye: and so neer blood has made us
With the dear love I ever bore your virtues
That I will be a Brother to your griefs too:
Be comforted, 'tis no dishonor Sister
To love, nor to love him you do: he is a Gentleman
Of as sweet hopes, as years, as many promises,
As there be growing Truths, and great ones.

THEODOSIA
O Sir!

PHILIPPO
Do not despair.

THEODOSIA
Can ye forgive?

PHILIPPO
Yes Sister,
Though this be no small error, a far greater.

THEODOSIA
And think me still your Sister?

PHILIPPO
My dear Sister.

THEODOSIA
And will you counsel me?

PHILIPPO
To your own peace too:
Ye shall love still.

THEODOSIA
How good ye are!

PHILIPPO
My business,
And duty to my Father: which now drew me
From Salamanca I will lay aside
And only be your Agent to perswade ye
To leave both love, and him, and well retire ye.

THEODOSIA
Oh gentle Brother.

PHILIPPO
I perceive 'tis folly:
Delaies in love, more dangerous.

THEODOSIA
Noble Brother.

PHILIPPO
Fear not, I'll run your own way: and to help you,
Love having rackt your passions beyond counsel:
I'll hazard mine own fame: whither shall we venture?

THEODOSIA
Alas, I know not Sir!

PHILIPPO
Come, 'tis bright morning
Let's walk out, and consider: you'll keep this habit.

THEODOSIA
I would Sir.

PHILIPPO
Then it shall be: what must I call ye?
Come, do not blush: pray speak, I may spoil all else.

THEODOSIA
Pray call me Theodoro.

[Enter **DIEGO**.

DIEGO
Are ye ready?
The day draws on apace: once more good morrow.

THEODOSIA
Good morrow gentle Host: now I must thank ye:

PHILIPPO
Who dost thou think this is?

DIEGO
Were you a wench Sir,
I think you would know before me.

PHILIPPO
Mine own Brother.

DIEGO
By th' Masse your noses are akin: should I then
Have been so barbarous to have parted Brothers?

PHILIPPO
You knew it then.

DIEGO
I knew 'twas necessary
You should be both together: Instinct Signior,
Is a great matter in an Host.

THEODOSIA
I am satisfied.

[Enter **PEDRO**.

PEDRO
Is not mine Host up yet?

PHILIPPO
Who's that?

DIEGO
I'll see.

PHILIPPO
Sister, withdraw your self.

[She retires.

PEDRO
Signior Philippo.

PHILIPPO
Noble Don Pedro, where have you been this way?

PEDRO
I came from Port St. Maries, whence the Gallies
Put this last tide, and bound for Barcelona,
I brought Mark-antonie upon his way.

PHILIPPO
Marc-antonie?

PEDRO
Who is turn'd Soldier,
And entertain'd in the new Regiment,
For Naples.

PHILIPPO
Is it possible?

PEDRO
I assure you.

PHILIPPO
And put they in at Barcelona?

PEDRO
So
One of the Masters told me.

PHILIPPO
Which way go you Sir?

PEDRO
Home.

PHILIPPO
And I for Sivil: pray you Sir; say not
That you saw me, if you shall meet the question,
I have some little business.

PEDRO
Were it less Sir.

It shall not become me, to lose the caution:
Shall we breakfast together?

PHILIPPO
I'll come to you Sir:

[Exit **PEDRO**.

Sister you hear this: I believe your fortune
Begins to be propitious to you: we will hire
Mules of mine Host here: if we can, himself
To be our guide, and straight to Barcelona,
This was as happy news, as unexpected
Stay you till I rid him away.

THEODOSIA
I will.

[Exeunt.

Enter **ALPHONSO** and a **SERVANT**.

ALPHONSO
Knock at the door.

SERVANT
'Tis open Sir.

ALPHONSO
That's all one,
Knock when I bid you.

SERVANT
Will not your Worship enter?

ALPHONSO
Will not you learn more manners Sir, and do that
Your Master bids ye; knock ye knave, or I'll knock
Such a round peal about your pate: I enter
Under his roof, or come to say god save ye
To him, the Son of whose base dealings has undone me?
Knock louder, louder yet:

[**SERVANT** knocks.

I'll starve, and rot first,
This open air is every mans.

2ND SERVANT [within]
Come in Sir.

[Enter Second **SERVANT**.

ALPHONSO
No, no Sir, I am none of these Come in Sirs,
None of those visitants: bid your wise Master
Come out, I have to talk unto him: go Sir.

2ND SERVANT
Your worship may be welcome.

ALPHONSO
Sir, I will not,
I come not to be welcome: good my three Duckets,
My pickell'd sprat a day, and no oil to't,
And once a year a cotten coat, leave prating
And tell your Master I am here.

2ND SERVANT
I will Sir.
This is a strange old man.

[Exit.

ALPHONSO
I welcome to him?
I'll be first welcome to a Pesthouse: Sirrah
Let's have your valour now cas'd up, and quiet
When an occasion calls, 'tis wisdom in ye,
A Servingman's discretion: if you do draw,

[Enter **LEONARDO**, and **DON SANCHIO**, carried by two **SERVANTS** in a chair.)

Draw but according to your entertainment;
Five Nobles worth of fury.

LEONARDO
Signior Alphonso,
I hope no discontent from my Will given,
Has made ye shun my house: I ever lov'd ye.

An credit me amongst my fears 'tis greatest
To minister offences.

ALPHONSO
O good Signior
I know ye for Italian breed, fair tongu'd,
Spare your Apologies, I care not for 'em,
As little for your love Sir; I can live
Without your knowledge, eat mine own, and sleep
Without dependences, or hopes upon ye.
I come to ask my Daughter.

LEONARDO
Gentle Sir.

ALPHONSO
I am not gentle Sir, nor gentle will be
Till I have justice, my poor child restor'd
Your caper-cutting boy has run away with.
Young Signior smooth-face, he that takes up wenches
With smiles, and sweet behaviors, Songs, and Sonnets,
Your high fed Jennet, that no hedge can hold
They say you bred him for a Stallion.

SANCHIO
Fie Signior, there be times, and terms of honor
To argue these things in, descidements able
To speak ye noble Gentlemen, ways punctual
And to the life of credit, ye are too rugged.

ALPHONSO
I am too tame Sir.

LEONARDO
Will ye hear but reason?

ALPHONSO
No, I will hear no reason: I come not hither
To be popt off with reason; reason then.

SANCHIO
Why Signior, in all things there must be method,
Ye choak the child of honor else, discretion,
Do you conceive an injury?

ALPHONSO
What then Sir?

SANCHIO
Then follow it in fair terms, let your sword bite
When time calls, not your tongue.

ALPHONSO
I know Sir
Both when and what to do without directions,
And where, and how, I come not to be tutor'd,
My cause is no mans but mine own: you Signior,
Will ye restore my Daughter?

LEONARDO
Who detains her?

ALPHONSO
No more of these slight shifts.

LEONARDO
Ye urge me Signior
With strange injustice: because my Son has err'd—

SANCHIO
Mark him.

LEONARDO
Out of the heat of youth: dos't follow
I must be father of his crimes?

ALPHONSO
I say still.
Leave off your Rhetorick, and restore my Daughter.
And suddainly: bring in your rebel too,
Mountdragon, he that mounts without commission
That I may see him punished, and severely,
Or by that holy Heaven, I'll fire your house,
And there's my way of honor.

SANCHIO
Pray give me leave
Was not man made the noblest creature?

ALPHONSO
Well Sir.

SANCHIO
Should not his mind then answer to his making,
And to his mind his actions, if this ought to be,
Why do we run a blind way from our worths,

And cancel our discretions, doing those things
To cure offences, are the most offences?
We have rules of justice in us; to those rules
Let us apply our angers: you can consider
The want in others of these terminations
And how unfurnish'd they appear.

ALPHONSO
Hang others,
And where the wrongs are open, hang respects,
I come not to consider.

LEONARDO
Noble Sir,
Let us argue cooly, and consider like men.

ALPHONSO
Like men!

LEONARDO
Ye are too sudain still.

ALPHONSO
Like men Sir?

SANCHIO
It is fair language, and ally'd to honor.

ALPHONSO
Why, what strange beast would your grave reverence
Make me appear? like men!

SANCHIO
Taste but that point Sir,
And ye recover all.

ALPHONSO
I tell thy wisdom
I am as much a man, and as good a man.

LEONARDO
All this is granted Sir.

ALPHONSO
As wise a man.

SANCHIO
Ye are not tainted that way.

ALPHONSO
And a man
Dares make thee no man; or at best, a base man.

SANCHIO
Fie, fie, here wants much carriage.

ALPHONSO
Hang much carriage.

LEONARDO
Give me good language.

ALPHONSO
Sirrah Signior, Give me my Daughter.

LEONARDO
I am as gentle as your self, as free born.

SANCHIO
Observe his way.

LEONARDO
As much respect ow'd to me.

SANCHIO
This hangs together nobly.

LEONARDO
And for Civil,
A great deal more it seems: go look your Daughter.

SANCHIO
There ye went well off Signior.

LEONARDO
That rough tongue
You understand at first: you never think Sir
Out of your mightiness, of my loss: here I stand
A patient Anvil, to your burning angers
Made subject to your dangers; yet my loss equal:
Who shall bring home my Son?

ALPHONSO
A whipping Beadle.

LEONARDO

Why, is your Daughter whorish?

ALPHONSO
Ha, thou dar'st not,
By heaven I know thou dar'st not.

LEONARDO
I dare more Sir
If you dare be uncivil.

ALPHONSO
Laugh too, Pidgeon.

SANCHIO
A fitter time for fames sake: two weak Nurses
Would laugh at this; are there no more days coming,
No ground but this to argue on? no swords left
Nor friends to carry this, but your own furies?
Alas! it shows too weakly.

ALPHONSO
Let it show,
I come not here for shews: laugh at me sirrah?
I'll give ye cause to laugh.

LEONARDO
Ye are as like sir
As any man in Spain.

ALPHONSO
By heaven I will,
I will brave Leonardo.

LEONARDO
Brave Alphonso.
I will expect it then.

SANCHIO
Hold ye there both,
These terms are noble.

ALPHONSO
Ye shall hear shortly from me.

SANCHIO
Now discreetly.

ALPHONSO

Assure your self ye shall: do ye see this sword sir?
He has not cast his teeth yet.

SANCHIO
Rarely carried.

ALPHONSO
He bites deep: most times mortal: Signior
I'll hound him at the fair and home.

SANCHIO
Still nobly.

ALPHONSO
And at all those that dare maintain ye.

SANCHIO
Excellent.

LEONARDO
How you shall please sir, so it be fair, though certain,
I had rather give you reason.

SANCHIO
Fairly urg'd too.

ALPHONSO
This is no age for reason; prick your reason
Upon your swords point.

SANCHIO
Admirably follow'd.

ALPHONSO
And there I'll hear it: so till I please, live Sir. Exit.

LEONARDO
And so farewel, you're welcome.

[Exit **ALPHONSO** with **1ˢᵗ SERVANT**.

SANCHIO
The end crowns all things
Signior, some little business past, this cause I'll argue
And be a peace between ye, if't so please ye,
And by the square of honor to the utmost:
I feel the old man's master'd by much passion,
And too high rackt, which makes him overshoot all

His valour should direct at, and hurt those
That stand but by as blenchers: this he must know too,
As necessary to his judgement, doting women
Are neither safe nor wise adventurers: conceive me,
If once their wills have wander'd; nor is't then
A time to use our rages: for why should I
Bite at the stone, when he that throws it wrongs me?
Do not we know that Women are most wooers
Though closest in their carriage? Do not all men know,
Scarce all the compass of the Globe can hold 'em
If their affections be afoot? shall I then covet
The follies of a she-fool, that by nature
Must seek her like, by reason, be a woman,
Sink a tall ship, because the sails defie me?
No, I disdain that folly; he that ventures
Whilst they are fit to put him on, has found out
The everlasting motion in his scabbard.
I doubt not to make peace: and so for this time
My best love, and remembrance.

LEONARDO
Your poor Servant.

[Exeunt.

SCÆNA SECUNDA

Enter **DIEGO**, **PHILIPPO** and **THEODOSIA**.

PHILIPPO
Where will our Horses meet us?

DIEGO
Fear not you Sir,
Some half mile hence my worships man will stay us,
How is it with my young bloods? come, be jovial,
Let's travel like a merry flock of wild Geese,
Every tongue talking.

PHILIPPO
We are very merry;
But do you know this way, Sir?

THEODOSIA
Is't not dangerous?
Methinks these woody thickets should harbor knaves.

DIEGO

I fear none but fair wenches; those are thieves,
May quickly rob me of my good conditions,
If they cry Stand once: but the best is Signiors
They cannot bind my hands: for any else,
They meet an equal knave, and there's my Passport:
I have seen fine sport in this place: had these three tongues,
They would tell ye pretty matters: do not you fear, though
They are not every daies delights.

PHILIPPO

What sport Sir?

DIEGO

Why to say true, the sport of all sports.

PHILIPPO

What was't?

DIEGO

Such turning up of Taffataes; and you know
To what rare whistling tunes they go, far beyond
A soft wind in the shrowds: such stand there,
And down i'th' other place; such supplications
And subdivisions for those toys their honors,
One, as ye are a Gentleman in this bush,
And oh sweet Sir, what mean ye? there's a bracelet,
And use me I beseech ye like a woman;
And her petition's heard: another scratches,
And cries she will die first, and then swounds: but certain
She is brought to life again, and does well after.
Another, save mine honor, oh mine honor,
My Husband serves the Duke, Sir, in his kitchen;
I have a cold pie for ye; fie, fie, fie Gentlemen,
Will nothing satisfie, where's my Husband?
Another cries, do ye see Sir how they use me,
Is there no Law for these things?

THEODOSIA

And good mine Host,
Do you call these fine sports?

DIEGO

What should I call 'em,
They have been so call'd these thousand years and upwards.

PHILIPPO

But what becomes o'th' men?

DIEGO
They're stript and bound,
Like so many Adams, with fig-leaves afore 'em,
And there's their innocence.

THEODOSIA
Would we had known this!
Before we reacht this place.

PHILIPPO
Come, there's no danger,
These are but sometimes chances.

DIEGO
Now we must through.

[Enter **INCUBO**, the **BAILIFF**.

THEODOSIA
Who's that?

DIEGO
Stand to it Signiors.

PHILIPPO
No it needs not,
I know the face; 'tis honest.

INCUBO
What mine Host:
Mine everlasting honest Host.

HOSTESS
Mass Baily:
Now in the name of an ill reckoning
What make you walking this round?

INCUBO
A pox of this round,
And of all business too, through woods, and rascals,
They have rounded me away a dozen Duckets,
Besides a fair round Cloak: Some of 'em knew me,
Else they had cased me like a Cunnie too,
As they have done the rest, and I think roasted me,
For they began to baste me soundly: my young Signiors,
You may thank heaven, and heartily, and hourly,

You set not out so early; ye had been smoak'd else
By this true hand ye had Sirs, finely smoak'd,
Had ye been Women, smockt too.

THEODOSIA
Heaven defend us.

INCUBO
Nay, that had been no prayer, there were those
That run that prayer out of breath, yet fail'd too.
There was a Fryer, now ye talk of prayer,
With a huge bunch of Beads, like a rope of Onions:
I am sure as big, that out of fear and prayer,
In halfe an hour, wore 'em as small as Bugles,
Yet he was flead too.

PHILIPPO
At what hour was this?

INCUBO
Some two hours since.

THEODOSIA
Do you think the passage sure now.

INCUBO
Yes, a rope take 'em, as it will, and bless 'em,
They have done for this day sure.

PHILIPPO
Are many rifled?

INCUBO
At the least a dozen,
And there left bound.

THEODOSIA
How came you free?

INCUBO
A curtesie
They use out of their rogueships, to bequeath
To one, that when they give a sign from far
Which is from out of danger; he may presently
Release the rest, as I met you, I was going,
Having the sign from yonder hill to do it.

THEODOSIA

Alas poor men.

PHILIPPO
Mine Host, pray go untie 'em.

DIEGO
Let me alone for cancelling: where are they?

INCUBO
In every bush, like black birds, you cannot miss 'em.

DIEGO
I need not stalk unto 'em.

INCUBO
No, they'l stand ye,
My busie life for yours Sir:

[Exit **DIEGO**.

You would wonder
To see the several tricks and strange behaviours
Of the poor rascals in their miseries,
One weeps, another laughs at him for weeping,
A third is monstrous angry, he can laugh
And cries, go too, this is no time; he laughs still,
A fourth exhorts to patience: him a fifth man
Curses for tameness; him a Fryer schools,
All hoot the Fryer, here one sings a Ballad,
And there a little Curate confutes him,
And in this linsey-woolsey way, that would make a dog
Forget his dinner, or an old man fire,
They rub out for their ransoms: Amongst the rest,
There is a little boy rob'd, a fine child,
It seems a Page: I must confess my pitty
(As 'tis a hard thing in a man of my place)
To shew compassion, stirr'd at him, so finely
And without noise he carries his afflictions,
And looks as if he had but dreamt of losing.

[Enter **DIEGO** and **LEOCADIA** disguised as a boy, a **FRIAR,** and others as rob'd.

This boy's the glory of this robbery,
The rest but shame the action: now ye may hear 'em.

DIEGO
Come lads, 'tis Holy-day: hang cloaths, 'tis hot,
And sweating Agues are abroad.

1ˢᵀ OTHER

It seems so;
For we have met with rare Physitians
To cure us of that malady.

DIEGO

Fine footing,
Light and deliver: now my boys: Master Fryer,
How does your Holiness, bear up man; what
A cup of neat Sack now and a toast: ha, Fryer,
A warm plaister to your belly Father,
There were a blessing now.

FRIAR

Ye say your mind Sir.

DIEGO

Where my fine Boy: my poynter.

INCUBO

There's the wonder.

DIEGO

A rank whore scratch their sides till the pox follow
For robbing thee, thou hast a thousand ways
To rob thy self boy, Dice, and a Chamber-Devil.

LEOCADIA

Ye are deceiv'd Sir.

DIEGO

And thy Master too boy.

PHILIPPO

A sweet-fac'd boy indeed: what rogues were these?
What barbarous, brutish slaves to strip this beauty?

THEODOSIA

Come hither my boy: alas! he's cold, mine Host,
We must intreat your Cloak.

DIEGO

Can ye intreat it.

PHILIPPO

We do presume so much, you have other garments.

DIEGO
Will you intreat those too?

THEODOSIA
Your Mule must too,
To the next Town, you say 'tis near: in pitty
You cannot see this poor Boy perish.
I know ye have a better soul, we'll satisfie ye.

DIEGO
'Tis a strange foolish trick I have, but I cannot help it,
I am ever cozen'd with mine own commendations;
It is determin'd then I shall be robb'd too.
To make up vantage to this dozen: here Sir,

[Giving his cloak to **LEOCADIA**.

Heaven has provided ye a simple garment
To set ye off: pray keep it handsomer
Than you kept your own; and let me have it render'd,
Brush'd and discreetly folded.

LEOCADIA
I thank ye Sir.

DIEGO
Who wants a Doublet?

2ND OTHER
I.

DIEGO
Where will you have it?

2ND OTHER
From you Sir, if you please.

DIEGO
Oh, there's the point, Sir.

PHILIPPO
My honest friends, I am sorry for your fortunes,
But that's but poor relief: here are ten Ducats,
And to your distribution, holy Sir,

[Giving money to **FRIAR**.

I render 'em: and let it be your care

To see 'em, as your wants are, well divided.

DIEGO
Plain dealing now my friends: and Father Fryer,
Set me the Sadle right; no wringing Fryer,
Nor tithing to the Church, these are no duties;
Scour me your conscience, if the Devil tempt ye
Off with your cord, and swinge him.

FRIAR
Ye say well Sir.

ALL
Heaven keep your goodness.

THEODOSIA
Peace keep you, farewel friends.

DIEGO
Farewel light-Horse-men.

[Exit the **FRIAR** and the **ROB'D**.

PHILIPPO
Which way travel you Sir.

INCUBO
To the next Town.

THEODOSIA
Do you want any thing.

INCUBO
Only discretion to travel at good hours,
And some warm meat to moderate this matter,
For I am most outragious cruel hungry.

DIEGO
I have a stomach too such as it is.
Would pose a right good pasty, I thank heaven for't.

INCUBO
Cheese, that would break the teeth of a new handsaw,
I could endure now like an Oastrich, or salt beef,
That Cesar left in pickel.

PHILIPPO
Take no care,

We'll have meat for you, and enough: I'th' mean time
Keep you the horse way, lest the fellow miss us,
We'll meet ye at the end o'th' wood.

DIEGO
Make haste then.

[Exit **DIEGO** and **INCUBO**.

THEODOSIA
My pretty Sir till your necessities
Be full supplied, so please you trust our friendships,
We must not part.

LEOCADIA
Ye have pull'd a charge upon ye,
Yet such a one as ever shall be thankful.

PHILIPPO
Ye have said enough, may I be bold to ask ye,
What Province you were bred in? and of what Parents?

LEOCADIA
Ye may Sir: I was born in Andaluzia,
My name Francisco, son to Don Henriques
De Cardinas.

THEODOSIA
Our noble neighbor.

PHILIPPO
Son to Don Henriques?
I know the Gentleman: and by your leave Sir,
I know he has no son.

LEOCADIA
None of his own Sir,
Which makes him put that right upon his Brother
Don Sanchio's children: one of which I am,
And therefore do not much err.

PHILIPPO
Still ye do Sir,
For neither has Don Sanchio any son;
A Daughter, and a rare one is his heir,
Which though I never was so blest to see,
Yet I have heard great good of.

THEODOSIA
Urge no further,
He is ashamed, and blushes.

PHILIPPO
Sir,
If it might import you to conceal your self,
I ask your mercy, I have been so curious:

LEOCADIA
Alas! I must ask yours Sir: for these lies,
Yet they were useful ones; for by the claiming
Such noble parents, I believ'd your bounties
Would shew more gracious: The plain truth is Gentlemen,
I am Don Sanchio's Stewards son, a wild boy,
That for the fruits of his unhappiness,
Is faign to seek the wars.

THEODOSIA
This is a lie too.
If I have any ears.

PHILIPPO
Why?

THEODOSIA
Mark his language,
And ye shall find it of too sweet a relish
For one of such a breed: I'll pawn my hand,
This is no boy.

PHILIPPO
No boy? what would you have him?

THEODOSIA
I know, no boy: I watcht how fearfully,
And yet how suddainly he cur'd his lies,
The right wit of a Woman: Now I am sure.

PHILIPPO
What are ye sure?

THEODOSIA
That 'tis no boy: I'll burn in't.

PHILIPPO
Now I consider better, and take council,
Methinks he shows more sweetness in that face,

Than his fears dare deliver.

THEODOSIA
No more talk on't,
There hangs some great weight by it: soon at night
I'll tell ye more.

PHILIPPO
Come Sir, what e'r you are
With us, embrace your liberty, and our helps
In any need you have.

LEOCADIA
All my poor service
Shall be at your command Sir, and my prayers.

PHILIPPO
Let's walk apace; hunger will cut their throats else.

[Exeunt.

SCÆNA TERTIA

On board a galley at sea

Enter **RODORIGO**, **MARK-ANTONIO** and a **SHIP-MASTER**, two Chairs set out.

RODRIGO
Call up the Master.

SHIP-MASTER
Here Sir.

RODRIGO
Honest Master,
Give order all the Gallies with this tyde
Fall round, and near upon us; that the next wind
We may weigh off together, and recover
The Port of Barcelona, without parting.

SHIP-MASTER
Your pleasure's done Sir.

[Exit.

RODRIGO

Signior Mark-antonio,
Till meat be ready, let's sit here and prepare
Our stomachs with discourses.

MARK-ANTONIO
What you please Sir.

[They sit.

RODRIGO
Pray ye answer me to this doubt.

MARK-ANTONIO
If I can Sir.

RODRIGO
Why should such plants as you are; pleasure children,
That owe their blushing years to gentle objects,
Tenderly bred, and brought up in all fulness,
Desire the stubborn wars?

MARK-ANTONIO
In those 'tis wonder,
That make their ease their god, and not their honor:
But noble General my end is other,
Desire of knowledge Sir, and hope of tying
Discretion to my time, which only shews me,
And not my years, a man, and makes that more
Which we call handsome, the rest is but Boys beauty,
And with the Boy consum'd.

RODRIGO
Ye argue well Sir.

MARK-ANTONIO
Nor do I wear my youth, as they wear breeches,
For object, but for use: my strength for danger,
Which is the liberal part of man, not dalliance,
The wars must be my Mistress Sir.

RODRIGO
Oh Signior,
You'll find her a rough wench.

MARK-ANTONIO
When she is won once,
She'll show the sweeter Sir.

RODRIGO
You can be pleas'd, though
Sometimes to take a tamer?

MARK-ANTONIO
'Tis a truth Sir,
So she be handsome, and not ill condition'd.

RODRIGO
A Soldier should not be so curious.

MARK-ANTONIO
I can make shift with any for a heat Sir.

RODRIGO
Nay, there you wrong your youth too: and however
You are pleas'd to appear to me, which shews well Signior,
A tougher soul than your few years can testifie:
Yet, my young Sir, out of mine own experience
When my spring was, I am able to confute ye,
And say, y' had rather come to th' shock of eies,
And boldly march up to your Mistriss mouth,
Then to the Cannons.

MARK-ANTONIO
That's as their lading is Sir.

RODRIGO
There be Trenches
Fitter and warmer for your years, and safer
Than where the bullet plaies.

MARK-ANTONIO
Ther's it I doubt Sir.

RODRIGO
You'll easily find that faith: But come, be liberal,
What kind of Woman, could you make best wars with?

MARK-ANTONIO
They are all but heavy marches.

RODRIGO
Fie Marckantonio,
Beauty in no more reverence?

MARK-ANTONIO
In the Sex Sir,

I honor it, and next to honor, love it,
For there is only beauty; and that sweetness
That was first meant for modesty: sever it
And put it in one woman, it appears not,
'Tis of too rare a nature, she too gross
To mingle with it.

RODRIGO
This is a meer heresie.

MARK-ANTONIO
Which makes 'em ever mending; for that gloss
That cozens us for beauty, is but bravery,
An outward shew of things well set, no more:
For heavenly beauty, is as heaven it self Sir,
Too excellent for object, and what is seen
Is but the vail then, airy clouds; grant this
It may be seen, 'tis but like stars in twinklings.

RODRIGO
'Twas no small study in their Libraries
Brought you to this experience: But what think ye
Of that fair red and white, which we call Beauty?

MARK-ANTONIO
Why? 'tis our creature Sir, we give it 'em,
Because we like those colours, else 'tis certain
A blew face with a motley nose would do it;
And be as great a beauty, so we lov'd it;
That we cannot give, which is only beauty,
Is a fair Mind.

RODRIGO
By this rule, all our choices
Are to no ends.

MARK-ANTONIO
Except the dull end, Doing.

RODRIGO
Then all to you seem equal?

MARK-ANTONIO
Very true Sir,
And that makes equal dealing: I love any
That's worth love.

RODRIGO

How long love ye Signior?

MARK-ANTONIO
Till I have other business.

RODRIGO
Do you never
Love stedfastly one woman?

MARK-ANTONIO
'Tis a toil Sir
Like riding in one rode perpetually,
It offers no variety.

RODRIGO
Right youth,
He must needs make a Soldier; nor do you think
One Woman, can love one man?

MARK-ANTONIO
Yes, that may be.
Though it appear not often; they are things ignorant,
And therefore apted to that superstition
Of doting fondness; yet of late years Signior,
That worlds well mended with 'em, fewer are found now
That love at length, and to the right mark, all
Stir now as the time stirs; fame and fashion
Are ends they aim at now, and to make that love
That wiser ages held ambition;
They that cannot reach this may love by Index;
By every days surveying who best promises,
Who has done best, who may do, and who mended
May come to do again: who appear nearest
Either in new stampt clothes; or courtesies,
Done but from hand to mouth neither; nor love they these things
Longer than new are making, nor that succession
Beyond the next fair feather: Take the City,
There they go to't by gold weight, no gain from 'em
All they can work by fire and water to 'em,
Profit is all they point at, if there be love
'Tis shew'd ye by so dark a light, to bear out
The bracks and old stains in it, that ye may purchase
French Velvet better cheap, all loves are endless.

RODRIGO
Faith, if you have a Mistriss, would she heard you.

MARK-ANTONIO

'Twere but the vent'ring of my place, or swearing
I meant it but for argument, as Schoolmen
Dispute high questions.

RODRIGO
What a world is this
When young men dare determine what those are
Age and the best experience ne'r could aim at.

MARK-ANTONIO
They were thick ey'd then Sir; now the print is bigger
And they may read their fortunes without spectacles.

RODRIGO
Did you ne'r love?

MARK-ANTONIO
Faith yes, once after supper,
And the fit held till midnight.

RODRIGO
Hot, or shaking.

MARK-ANTONIO
To say true, both.

RODRIGO
How did ye rid it?

MARK-ANTONIO
Thus Sir,
I laid my hand upon my heart, and blest me
And then said over certain charms I had learn'd
Against mad dogs, for love and they are all one;
Last thought upon a windmil, and so slept,
And was well ever after.

RODRIGO
A rare Physitian,
What would your practise gain ye?

MARK-ANTONIO
The wars ended,
I mean to use my Art, and have these fools
Cut in the head like Cats, to save the kingdom,
Another Inquisition.

RODRIGO

So old a Soldier
Out of the wars, I never knew yet practised.

MARK-ANTONIO
I shall mend every day; but noble General,
Believe this, but as this you nam'd discourses.

RODRIGO
Oh ye are a cunning Gamester.

MARK-ANTONIO
Mirths and toys
To cosin time withal, for o' my troth Sir,
I can love; I think, well too; well enough
And think as well of women as they are,
Pretty fantastick things, some more regardful,
And some few worth a service: I am so honest,
I wish 'em all in heaven, and you know how hard Sir
'Twill be to get in there with their great farthingals.

RODRIGO
Well Mark-antonio, I would not loose thy company
For the best Galley I command.

MARK-ANTONIO
Faith General,
If these discourses please ye, I shall fit ye
Once every day.

[Knock within.

RODRIGO
Thou canst not please me better: hark, they call
Below to dinner: ye are my Cabbin guest,
My bosom's, so you please Sir.

MARK-ANTONIO
Your poor Servant.

[Exeunt.

SCÆNA QUARTA.

A Roon in an Inn.

Enter **HOST** and his **WIFE**.

HOST

Let 'em have meat enough Woman, half a Hen;
There be old rotten Pilchards, put 'em off too,
'Tis but a little new anointing of 'em.
And a strong onion, that confounds the stink.

WIFE

They call for more Sir.

HOST

Knock a dozen eggs down,
But then beware your wenches.

WIFE

More than this too?

HOST

Worts, worts, and make 'em porridge: pop 'em up wench
But they shall pay for Cullyses.

WIFE

All this is nothing;
They call for Kid and Partridge.

HOST

Well remembred,
Where's the Faulconers half dog he left?

WIFE

It stinks Sir,
Past all hope that way.

HOST

Run it o'r with Garlick,
And make a Roman dish on't.

WIFE

Pray ye be patient,
And get provision in; these are fine gentlemen,
And liberal gentlemen; they have unde quare
No mangey Muleters, nor pinching Posts,
That feed upon the parings of Musk-millions
And Radishes, as big and tough as Rafters:
Will ye be stirring in this business? here's your brother,
Mine old Host of Ossuna, as wise as you are,
That is, as knavish; if ye put a trick,
Take heed he do not find it.

HOST
I'll be wagging.

WIFE
'Tis for your own commodity: why wenches!

[Exit **HOST**.

SERVANT [within]
Anon forsooth.

WIFE
Who makes a fire there? and who gets in water?
Let Oliver goe to the Justice, and beseech his Worship
We may have two spits going; and do you hear Druce,
Let him invite his Worship, and his Wives Worship,
To the left-Meat to morrow.

[Enter **INCUBO**.

INCUBO
Where's this Kitchen?

WIFE
Even at the next door Signior: what old Don?
We meet but seldom.

INCUBO
Prethee be patient Hostess,
And tell me where the meat is.

WIFE
Faith Master Baylie,
How have ye done? and how man?

INCUBO
Good sweet Hostess,
What shall we have to dinner?

WIFE
How does your woman,
And a fine Woman she is, and a good Woman;
Lord, how you bear your years!

INCUBO
Is't Veal or Mutton,
Beef, Bacon, Pork, Kid, Pheasant, or all these,

And are they ready all?

WIFE
The hours that have been
Between us two, the merry hours: Lord!

INCUBO
Hostess,
Dear Hostess do but hear; I am hungry.

WIFE
Ye are merrily dispos'd Sir.

INCUBO
Monstrous hungry,
And hungry after much meat, I have brought hither
Right worshipful to pay the reckoning,
Money enough too with 'em, desire enough
To have the best meat, and of that enough too:
Come to the point sweet wench, and so I kiss thee.

WIFE
Ye shall have any thing, and instantly
E'r you can lick your ears, Sir.

INCUBO
Portly meat,
Bearing substantial stuff, and fit for hunger
I do beseech ye Hostess first, then some light garnish,
Two Pheasants in a dish, if ye have Leverits,
Rather for way of ornament, than appetite
They may be look'd upon, or Larks: for Fish,
As there is no great need, so I would not wish ye
To serve above four dishes, but those full ones;
Ye have no Cheese of Parma?

WIFE
Very old Sir.

INCUBO
The less will serve us, some ten pound.

WIFE
Alas Sir,
We have not halfe these dainties.

INCUBO
Peace good Hostess,

And make us hope ye have.

WIFE
Ye shall have all Sir,

INCUBO
That may be got for money.

[Enter **DIEGO** and a **BOY**.

DIEGO
Where's your Master?
Bring me your Master, Boy: I must have liquor
Fit for the Mermydons; no dashing now child
No conjurings by candle light, I know all;
Strike me the oldest Sack, a piece that carries
Point blank to this place boy, and batters; Hostess,
I kiss thy hands through which many a round reckoning
And things of moment have had motion.

WIFE
Still mine old Brother.

DIEGO
Set thy Seller open,
For I must enter, and advance my Colours,
I have brought thee Dons indeed wench, Dons with Duckets
And those Dons must have dainty Wine, pure Bacchus
That bleeds the life blood: what is your cure ended?

INCUBO
We shall have Meat man.

DIEGO
Then we will have Wine man,
And Wine upon Wine, cut and drawn with Wine.

WIFE
Ye shall have all, and more than all.

INCUBO
All, well then.

DIEGO
Away, about your business, you with her
For old acquaintance sake, to stay
your stomach.

[Exit **WIFE** and **INCUBO**.

And Boy, be you my guide, ad inferos,
For I will make a full descent in equipage.

BOY
I'll shew you rare Wine.

DIEGO
Stinging geer?

BOY
Divine Sir.

DIEGO
O divine boy, march, march my child, rare Wine boy.

BOY
As any is in Spain Sir.

DIEGO
Old; and strong too,
Oh my fine boy, clear too?

BOY
As Christal Sir, and strong as truth.

DIEGO
Away boy,
I am enamor'd, and I long for Dalliance,
Stay no where child, not for thy fathers blessing,
I charge thee not to save thy Sisters honor,
Nor to close thy Dames eies, were she a dying
Till we arrive, and for thy recompence
I will remember thee in my Will.

BOY
Ye have said Sir.

[Exeunt.

ACTUS TERTIUS

SCÆNA PRIMA

Enter **PHILIPPO** and **HOST**.

PHILIPPO
Mine Host, is that Apparel got ye spoke of?
Ye shall have ready money.

HOST
'Tis come in, Sir, he has it on Sir
And I think 'twill be fit, and o' my credit
'Twas never worn but once Sir, and for necessity
Pawn'd to the man I told ye of.

PHILIPPO
Pray bargain for it,
And I will be the pay-master.

HOST
I will Sir.

PHILIPPO
And let our meat be ready when you please,
I mean as soon.

HOST
It shall be presently.

PHILIPPO
How far stands Barcelona?

HOST
But two Leagues off Sir,
You may be there by three a clock.

PHILIPPO
I am glad on't.

[Exeunt.

SCÆNA SECUNDA

Enter **THEODOSIA** and **LEOCADIA**.

THEODOSIA
Signior Francisco, why I draw you hither
To this remote place, marvel not, for trust me
My innocence yet never knew ill dealing,
And as ye have a noble temper, start not

Into offence, at any thing my knowledge,
And for your special good, would be inform'd of,
Nor think me vainly curious.

LEOCADIA
Worthy Sir,
The courtesies you and your noble Brother,
Even then when few men find the way to do 'em,
I mean in want, so freely showr'd upon me,
So truly, and so timely minister'd,
Must, if I should, suspect those minds that made 'em,
Either proclaim me an unworthy taker,
Or worse, a base beleever; Speek your mind Sir
Freely, and what you please, I am your Servant.

THEODOSIA
Then my young Sir know, since our first acquaintance
Induc'd by circumstances that deceive not
To clear some doubts I have; nay blush not Signior,
I have beheld ye narrowly: more blushes.
Sir, ye give me so much light, I find ye
A thing confest already: yet more blushes?
You would ill cover an offence might sink ye
That cannot hide your self; why do ye shake so?
I mean no trouble to ye; this fair hand
Was never made for hardness, nor those eies
(Come do not hide 'em,) for rough objects, harke ye,
Ye have betraid your self, that sigh confirms me;
Another? and a third too? then I see
These boys cloths do but pinch ye, come, be liberal,
Ye have found a friend that has found you, disguise not
That loaden soul that labors to be open:
Now you must weep, I know it, for I see
Your eies down laden to the lids, another
Manifest token that my doubts are perfect;
Yet I have found a greater; tell me this
Why were these holes left open, there was an error,
A foul one my Francisco, have I caught ye?
Oh pretty Sir, the custom of our Countrey
Allows men none in this place: Now the show'r comes.

LEOCADIA
Oh Signior Theodoro.

[Weeps.

THEODOSIA
This sorrow shows so sweetly

I cannot choose but keep it company:
Take truce and speak Sir: and I charge your goodness
By all those perfect hopes that point at virtue
By that remembrance these fair tears are shed for,
If any sad misfortune have thus form'd ye,
That either care or counsel may redeem,
Pain, purse, or any thing within the power
And honor of free gentlemen, reveal it,
And have our labors.

LEOCADIA
I have found ye noble
And ye shall find me true; your doubts are certain,
Nor dare I more dissemble; I am a woman,
The great example of a wretched woman.
Here you must give me leave to shew my sex;
And now to make ye know how much your credit
Has won upon my soul, so it please your patience,
I'll tell you my unfortunate sad story.

THEODOSIA
Sit down and say on Lady:

[They sit.

LEOCADIA
I am born Sir
Of good and honest parents, rich, and noble,
And not to lie, the Daughter of Don Sanchio,
If my unhappy fortune have not lost me:
My name call'd Leocadia, even the same
Your worthy brother did the special honor
To name for beautiful; and without pride
I have been often made believe so Signior;
But that's impertinent: Now to my sorrows;
Not far from us a Gentleman of worth,
A neighbor and a noble visitor,
Had his abode; who often met my Father
In gentle sports of Chase, and River-Hawking
In Course and Riding; and with him often brought
A Son of his, a young and hopeful Gentleman,
Nobly train'd up, in years fit for affection,
A sprightly man, of understanding excellent,
Of speech and civil 'haviour, no less powerful;
And of all parts, else my eies lied, abundant:
We grew acquainted, and from that acquaintance
Nearer into affection; from affection
Into belief.

THEODOSIA
Well.

LEOCADIA
Then we durst kiss.

THEODOSIA
Go forward.

LEOCADIA
But oh, man, man, unconstant, careless man,
Oh subtle man, how many are thy mischiefs;
Oh Mark-antonio, I may curse those kisses.

THEODOSIA
What did you call him Lady?

LEOCADIA
Mark-Antonio
The name to me of misery.

THEODOSIA
Pray foreward.

LEOCADIA
From these we bred desires sir; but lose me heaven
If mine were lustful.

THEODOSIA
I believe.

LEOCADIA
This nearness
Made him importunate; When to save mine honor
Love having full possession of my powers,
I got a Contract from him.

THEODOSIA
Sealed?

LEOCADIA
And sworn too;
Which since, for some offence heaven laid upon me,
I lost among my monies in the robbery,
The loss that makes me poorest: this won from him
Fool that I was, and too too credulous,
I pointed him a by-way to my chamber

The next night at an hour.

THEODOSIA
Pray stay there Lady;
And when the night came, came he, kept he touch with ye?
Be not so shamefac'd; had ye both your wishes?
Tell me, and tell me true, did he enjoy ye,
Were ye in one anothers arms abed? the Contract
Confirm'd in full joys there? did he lie with ye?
Answer to that; ha? did your father know this,
The good old man, or kindred privy to't?
And had ye their consents? did that nights promise
Make ye a Mother?

LEOCADIA
Why do you ask so nearly?
Good Sir, do's it concern you any thing?

THEODOSIA
No Lady.
Only the pitty why you should be used so
A little stirs me, but did he keep his promise?

LEOCADIA
No, no Signior,
Alas he never came, nor never meant it,
My Love was fool'd, time numbred to no end,
My expectation flouted, and ghesse you Sir,
What dor unto a doating Maid this was,
What a base breaking off!

THEODOSIA
All's well then Lady;
Go forward in your Story.

LEOCADIA
Not only fail'd Sir
Which is a curse in Love, and may he find it
When his affections are full-wing'd, and ready
To stoop upon the quarry, then when all
His full hopes are in's arms: not only thus Sir
But more injurious, faithless, treacherous,
Within two daies fame gave him far remov'd
With a new love, which much against my conscience
But more against my cause, which is my hell
I must confess a fair one, a right fair one,
Indeed of admirable sweetness, Daughter
Unto another of our noble neighbors

The thief call'd Theodosia; whose perfections
I am bound to ban for ever, curse to wrinckles,
As heaven I hope will make 'em soon; and aches;
For they have rob'd me poor unhappy wench
Of all, of all Sir, all that was my glory
And left me nothing but these tears, and travel:
Upon this certain news, I quit my Father
And if you be not milder in construction
I fear mine honour too: and like a Page
Stole to Ossuna, from that place to Sivil,
From thence to Barcelona I was travelling
When you o'er-took my misery, in hope to hear of
Gallies bound up for Italy; for never
Will I leave off the search of this bad man
This filcher of affections, this love-Pedler,
Nor shall my curses cease to blast her beauties
And make her name as wandring as her nature
Till standing face to face before their lusts
I call heavens justice down.

THEODOSIA
This shows too angry
Nor can it be her fault she is belov'd,
If I give meat, must they that eat it surfeit?

LEOCADIA
She loves again Sir, there's the mischief of it
And in despight of me to drown my blessings
Which she shall dearly know.

THEODOSIA
Ye are too violent.

LEOCADIA
She has Devils in her eyes, to whose devotion
He offers all his service.

THEODOSIA
Who can say
But she may be forsaken too? he that once wanders
From such a perfect sweetness, as you promise
Has he not still the same rule to deceive?

LEOCADIA
No, no they are together, love together
Past all deceit of that side; sleep together,
Live, and delight together, and such deceipt
Give me in a wild desert.

THEODOSIA

By your leave Lady
I see no honour in this cunning.

LEOCADIA

Honour?
True, none of her part, honour, she deserves none,
'Tis ceas'd with wandring Ladies such as she is,
So bold and impudent.

THEODOSIA

I could be angry
Extreamly angry now beyond my nature
And 'twere not for my pitty: what a man
Is this to do these wrongs: believe me Lady
I know the maid, and know she is not with him.

LEOCADIA

I would you knew she were in heaven.

THEODOSIA

And so well know her
That I think you are cozen'd.

LEOCADIA

So I say Sir.

THEODOSIA

I mean in her behaviour
For trust my faith so much I dare adventure for her credit
She never yet delighted to do wrong.

LEOCADIA

How can she then delight in him? dare she think?
Be what she will, as excellent as Angels
My love so fond, my wishes so indulgent
That I must take her prewnings; stoop at that
She has tyr'd upon; No Sir, I hold my beauty
Wash but these sorrows from it, of a sparkle
As right and rich as hers, my means as equal,
My youth as much unblown; and for our worths
And weight of virtue—

THEODOSIA

Do not task her so far.

LEOCADIA

By heaven she is cork, and clouds, light, light Sir, vapor
But I shall find her out, with all her witchcrafts,
Her paintings, and her powncings: for 'tis art
And only art preserves her, and meer spels
That work upon his powers; let her but shew me
A ruin'd cheek like mine, that holds his colour
And writes but sixteen years in spight of sorrows
An unbathed body, smiles, that give but shaddows,
And wrinkle not the face; besides she is little,
A demy dame, that makes no object.

THEODOSIA
Nay.
Then I must say you err; for credit me
I think she is taller than your self.

LEOCADIA
Why let her
It is not that shall mate me; I but ask
My hands may reach unto her.

THEODOSIA
Gentle Lady
'Tis now ill time of farther argument,
For I perceive your anger voyd of counsel,
Which I could wish more temperate.

LEOCADIA
Pray forgive me
If I have spoken uncivilly: they that look on
See more than we that play: and I beseech ye
Impute it loves offence, not mine; whose torments,
If you have ever lov'd, and found my crosses
You must confess are seldom ty'd to patience,
Yet I could wish I had said less.

THEODOSIA
No harm then;
Ye have made a full amends; our company
You may command, so please you in your travels
With all our faith and furtherance; let it be so.

LEOCADIA
Ye make too great an offer.

THEODOSIA
Then it shall be.
Go in and rest your self, our wholsome dyet

Will be made ready straight: But heark ye Lady
One thing I must entreat, your leave, and sufferance
That these things may be open to my Brother
For more respect and honor.

LEOCADIA
Do your pleasure.

THEODOSIA
And do not change this habit by no means
Unless ye change your self.

LEOCADIA
Which must not yet be.

THEODOSIA
It carries ye concealed and safe.

LEOCADIA
I am counsell'd.

[Exit.

[Enter **PHILIPPO**.

PHILIPPO
What's done?

THEODOSIA
Why all we doubted; 'tis a woman,
And of a noble strain too, ghess.

PHILIPPO
I cannot.

THEODOSIA
You have heard often of her.

PHILIPPO
Stay I think not.

THEODOSIA
Indeed ye have; 'tis the fair Leocadia
Daughter unto Don Sanchio, our noble neighbor.

PHILIPPO
Nay?

THEODOSIA
'Tis she Sir, o' my credit.

PHILIPPO
Leocadia,
Pish Leocadia, it must not be.

THEODOSIA
It must be, or be nothing.

PHILIPPO
Pray give me leave to wonder, Leocadia?

THEODOSIA
The very same.

PHILIPPO
The Damsel Leocadia
I ghest it was a woman, and a fair one
I see it through her shape, transparent plain
But that it should be she; tell me directly.

THEODOSIA
By heavens 'tis she.

PHILIPPO
By heaven then 'tis a sweet one.

THEODOSIA
That's granted too.

PHILIPPO
But heark ye, heark ye Sister,
How came she thus disguis'd?

THEODOSIA
I'll tell you that too
As I came on the self-same ground, so us'd too.

PHILIPPO
By the same man?

THEODOSIA
The same too.

PHILIPPO
As I live
You lovers have fine fancies,

Wonderous fine ones.

THEODOSIA
Pray heaven you never make one.

PHILIPPO
Faith I know not,
But in that mind I am, I had rather cobble,
'Tis a more Christian Trade; pray tell me one thing
Are not you two now monstrous jealous
Of one another?

THEODOSIA
She is much of me
And has rayl'd at me most unmercifully
And to my face, and o' my conscience
Had she but known me, either she or I
Or both, had parted with strange faces
She was in such a fury.

PHILIPPO
Leocadia?
Do's she speak handsomly?

THEODOSIA
Wondrous well Sir
And all she do's becomes her, even her anger.

PHILIPPO
How seemed she when you found her?

THEODOSIA
Had you seen
How sweetly fearful her pretty self
Betray'd her self, how neat her sorrow show'd,
And in what handsome phrase she put her story,
And as occasion stirr'd her how she started
Though roughly, yet most aptly into anger
You would have wonder'd.

PHILIPPO
Do's she know ye?

THEODOSIA
No,
Nor must not by no means.

PHILIPPO

How stands your difference?

THEODOSIA
I'll tell ye that some fitter time, but trust me
My Mark-Antonio has too much to answer.

PHILIPPO
May I take knowledge of her?

THEODOSIA
Yes she is willing.

PHILIPPO
Pray use her as she is, with all respects then,
For she is a woman of a noble breeding.

THEODOSIA
Ye shall not find me wanting.

PHILIPPO
Which way bears she?

THEODOSIA
Our way, and to our end.

PHILIPPO
I am glad on't; hark ye,
She keeps her shape?

[Enter **LEOCADIA**.

THEODOSIA
Yes, and I think by this time
Has mew'd her old.

PHILIPPO
She is here: by heaven a rare one,
An admirable sweet one, what an eye
Of what a full command she bears, how gracious
All her aspect shows; bless me from a feaver
I am not well o'th suddain.

LEOCADIA
Noble friends
Your meat and all my service waits upon ye.

PHILIPPO
Ye teach us manners Lady; all which service

Must now be mine to you, and all too poor too;
Blush not, we know ye, for by all our faiths
With us your honor is in sanctuary
And ever shall be.

LEOCADIA
I do well believe it,
Will ye walk nearer Sir.

[Exit.

THEODOSIA
She shows still fairer,
Yonger in every change, and clearer, neater;
I know not, I may fool my self, and finely
Nourish a wolfe to eat my heart out; certain
As she appears now, she appears a wonder,
A thing amazes me; what would she do then
In womans helps, in ornaments apt for her
And deckings to her delicacy? without all doubt
She would be held a miracle; nor can I think
He has forsaken her: Say what she please,
I know his curious eye, or say he had,
Put case he could be so boy-blind and foolish,
Yet stil I fear she keeps the Contract with her
Not stoln as she affirms, nor lost by negligence,
She would loose her self first, 'tis her life, and there
All my hopes are dispatch'd; O noble love
That thou couldst be without this jealousie,
Without this passion of the heart, how heavenly
Wouldst thou appear unto us? Come what may come
I'll see the end on't: and since chance has cast her
Naked into my refuge, all I can
She freely shall command, except the man.

[Exit.

SCÆNA TERTIA

Before the house of Leonardo.

Enter **LEONARDO** and **PEDRO**.

LEONARDO
Don Pedro do you think assuredly
The Galleys will come round to Barcelona

Within these two days?

PEDRO
Without doubt.

LEONARDO
And think ye
He will be with 'em certainly?

PEDRO
He is sir
I saw him at their setting off.

LEONARDO
Must they needs
Touch there for water as you say?

PEDRO
They must sir
And for fresh meat too, few or none go by it.
Beside so great a Fleet must needs want trimming
If they have met with fowl seas, and no harbor
On this side Spain, is able without danger
To moore 'em, but that haven.

LEONARDO
Are the wars
His only end?

PEDRO
So he professes.

LEONARDO
Bears he
Any command amongst 'em?

PEDRO
Good regard
With all; which quickly will prefer him.

LEONARDO
Pray Sir tell me,
And as you are a Gentleman be liberal.

PEDRO
I will Sir, and most true.

LEONARDO

Who saw ye with him?

PEDRO
None but things like himself; young Souldiers
And Gentlemen desirous to seek honor.

LEONARDO
Was there no woman there, nor none disguis'd
That might be thought a woman in his language?
Did he not let slip something of suspition
Touching that wanton way.

PEDRO
Believe me Sir
I neither saw, nor could suspect that face
That might be doubted womans, yet I am sure
Aboard him I see all that past, and 'tis impossible
Among so many high set bloods there should be
A woman, let her close her self within a cockle,
But they would open her, he must not love
Within that place alone, and therefore surely
He would not be so foolish had he any,
To trust her there; for his discourse, 'twas ever
About his business, war, or mirth to make us
Relish a Can of Wine well; when he spoke private
'Twas only the remembrance of his service,
And hope of your good prayers for his health Sir,
And so I gave him to the seas.

LEONARDO
I thank ye,
And now am satisfied, and to prevent
Suspitions that may nourish dangers Signior,
For I have told you how the mad Alphonso
Chafes like a Stag i'th toyl, and bends his fury
'Gainst all but his own ignorance; I am determin'd
For peace sake and the preservation
Of my yet untoucht honor, and his cure
My self to seek him there, and bring him back
As testimony of an unsought injury
By either of our actions; That the world,
And he if he have reason, may see plainly
Opinion is no perfect guide; nor all fames
Founders of truths: In the mean time this courtesie
I must intreat of you Sir, Be my self here
And as my self command my family.

PEDRO

Ye lay too much trust on me.

LEONARDO
'Tis my love Sir,
I will not be long from ye; if this question
Chance to be call'd upon ere my return
I leave your care to answer; so Farewell Sir.

PEDRO
Ye take a wise way; All my best endeavors
Shall labor in your absence; peace go with ye.

[Exit **LEONARDO**.

A noble honest Gentleman, free hearted
And of an open faith, much loving, and much loved,
And father of that goodness only malice
Can truly stir against, what dare befall
Till his return I'll answer.

[Exit **PEDRO**.

[Enter **ALPHONSO** and **SERVANT**.

ALPHONSO
Walk off Sirrah,
But keep your self within my call.

SERVANT
I will Sir.

ALPHONSO
And stir my horse for taking cold: within there!

[Exit **SERVANT**.

Hoa people; you that dwell there my brave Signior
What are ye all a sleep? is't that time with ye?

[Knocks.

I'll ring a little lowder.

[Knokcs.

[Enter **PEDRO**.

PEDRO

Sir who seek ye?

ALPHONSO
Not you Sir; Where's your Master?

PEDRO
I serve no man
In way of pay Sir.

ALPHONSO
Where's the man o'th house then?

PEDRO
What would you have with him Sir?

ALPHONSO
Do you stand here Sir
To ask men questions when they come?

PEDRO
I would sir
Being his friend, and hearing such alarmes
Know how men come to visit him.

ALPHONSO
Ye shall Sir,
Pray tell his mightiness here is a Gentleman
By name Alphonso, would intreat his conference
About affairs of State Sir, are ye answer'd?

[Enter **SANCHIO** carried.

PEDRO
I must be Sir.

SANCHIO
Stay, set me down, stay Signior,
You must stay, and ye shall stay.

ALPHONSO
Meaning me Sir?

SANCHIO
Yes you Sir, you I mean, I mean you.

ALPHONSO
Well Sir.
Why should I stay?

SANCHIO
There's reason.

ALPHONSO
Reason Sir?

SANCHIO
I reason Sir
My wrong is greatest, and I will be served first,
Call out the man of fame!

ALPHONSO
How serv'd Sir?

SANCHIO
Thus sir.

ALPHONSO
But not before me.

SANCHIO
Before all the world sir
As my case stands.

ALPHONSO
I have lost a daughter sir.

SANCHIO
I have lost another worth five score of her sir.

ALPHONSO
Ye must not tell me so.

SANCHIO
I have, and haerk ye?
Make it up five score more: Call out the fellow,
And stand you by sir.

PEDRO
This is the mad morriss.

ALPHONSO
And I stand by?

SANCHIO
I say stand by, and do it.

ALPHONSO
Stand by among thy lungs.

SANCHIO
Turn presently
And say thy prayers, thou art dead.

ALPHONSO
I scorn thee
And scorn to say my prayers more than thou do'st,
Mine is the most wrong, and my daughter dearest
And mine shall first be righted.

SANCHIO
Shall be righted.

PEDRO
A third may live I see, pray hear me Gentlemen.

SANCHIO
Shall be.

ALPHONSO
I, shall be righted.

SANCHIO
Now?

ALPHONSO
Now.

SANCHIO
Instantly.

ALPHONSO
Before I stir.

SANCHIO
Before me.

ALPHONSO
Before any.

SANCHIO
Dost thou consider what thou say'st? hast thou friends here
Able to quench my anger, or perswade me
After I have beaten thee into one main bruist
And made thee spend thy state in rotten apples,

Thou canst at length be quiet, shall I kill thee
Divide thee like a rotten Pumpion,
And leave thee stincking to posterity,
There's not the least blow I shall give; but do's this
Urge me no farther: I am first.

ALPHONSO
I'll hang first.
No goodman glory, 'tis not your bravado's,
Your punctual honor, nor soldadoship.

SANCHIO
Set me a little nearer.

ALPHONSO
Let him sally.
Lin'd with your quircks of carriage and discretion
Can blow me off my purpose. Where's your credit
With all your school points now? your decent arguing
And apt time for performing: where are these toys,
These wise ways, and most honorable courses,
To take revenge? how dar'st thou talk of killing,
Or think of drawing any thing but squirts
When letchery has dry founded thee?

SANCHIO
Neerer yet,
That I may spit him down: thou look'st like a man.

PEDRO
I would be thought so Sir.

SANCHIO
Prethee do but take me,
And fling me upon that Puppy.

ALPHONSO
Do for heavens sake,
And see but how I'll hug him.

SANCHIO
Yet take warning.

PEDRO
Faith Gentlemen, this is a needless quarrel.

SANCHIO
And do you desire to make one?

PEDRO
As a friend Sir,
To tell you all this anger is but lost Sir,
For Leonardo is from home.

ALPHONSO
No, no Sir.

PEDRO
Indeed he is.

SANCHIO
Where dare he be, but here Sir,
When men are wrong'd, and come for satisfactions.

PEDRO
It seems he has done none Sir; for his business
Clear of those cares, hath carried him for sometime
To Barcelona: if he had been guilty,
I know he would have stayd, and clear'd all difference
Either by free confession, or his sword.

SANCHIO
This must not be.

PEDRO
Sure as I live, it is Sir.

ALPHONSO
Sure, as we all live,
He's run away for ever: Barcelona!
Why? 'tis the key for Italy, from whence
He stole first hither.

SANCHIO
And having found his knaveries
Too gross to be forgiven, and too open,
He has found the same way back again: I believe too
The good grass Gentleman, for his own ease,
Has taken one o'th' Fillyes: Is not his stuff sold.

ALPHONSO
I fear his worships shoos too; to escape us,
I do not think he has a dish within doors,
A louse left of his linnage.

PEDRO

Ye are too wide Sir.

ALPHONSO
Or one poor wooden spoon.

PEDRO
Come in and see Sir.

ALPHONSO
I'll see his house on fire first.

PEDRO
Then be pleased Sir
To give better censure.

SANCHIO
I will after him,
And search him like conceal'd land, but I'll have him,
And though I find him in his shrift, I'll kill him.

ALPHONSO
I'll bear ye company.

SANCHIO
Pray have a care then,
A most especiall care, indeed a fear,
Ye do not anger me.

ALPHONSO
I will observe ye,
And if I light upon him handsomly.

SANCHIO
Kill but a piece of him, leave some Alphonso
For your poor Friends.

PEDRO
I fear him not for all this.

ALPHONSO
Shall we first go home,
For it may prove a voyage, and dispose
Of things there; heaven knows what may follow.

SANCHIO
No,
I'll kill him in this shirt I have on: let things
Govern themselves, I am master of my honor

At this time, and no more; let wife, and land,
Lie lay till I return.

ALPHONSO
I say amen to't:
But what care for our monies?

SANCHIO
I will not spend
Above three shillings, till his head be here,
Four is too great a sum for all his Fortunes.
Come take me up instantly.

ALPHONSO
Farewell to you Sir,
And if your friend be in a featherbed,
Sow'd up to shroud his fears, tell him 'tis folly,
For no course but his voluntary hanging
Can get our pardons.

[Exeunt.

PEDRO
These I think would be
Offence enough, if their own indiscretions
Would suffer 'em: two of the old seditious,
When they want enemies, they are their own foes:
Were they a little wiser, I should doubt 'em:
Till when I'll ne'r break sleep, nor suffer hunger
For any harm he shall receive: for 'tis as easie
If he be guilty, to turn these two old men
Upon their own throats, and look on, and live still,
As 'tis to tell five pound: a great deal sooner,
And so I'll to my meat, and then to hawking.

[Exit.

ACTUS QUARTUS

SCÆNA PRIMA

Enter **MARK-ANTONIO** and a **GENTLEMAN**.

MARK-ANTONIO
Sir, this is complement; I pray you leave me.

GENTLEMAN
Sir, it is not.

MARK-ANTONIO
Why? I would only see the Town.

GENTLEMAN
And only that I come to shew you.

MARK-ANTONIO
Which I can see without you.

GENTLEMAN
So you may
Plainly, not safely: For such difference
As you have seen betwixt the sea and earth
When waves rise high, and land would beat 'em back
As fearful of Invasion; such we find
When we land here at Barcelona.

MARK-ANTONIO
Sir.

GENTLEMAN
Besides our General of the Galleys, fearing
Your hasty nature, charg'd me not return
Without you safe.

MARK-ANTONIO
O Sir, that Roderigo
Is noble, and do's mistake my temper.
There is not in the world, a mind less apt
To conceive wrongs, or do 'em; has he seen me
In all this voyage, in the which he pleases.

[Enter **EUGENIA** with divers **ATTENDANTS**.

To call me friend, let slip a hasty word?
S'light Sir: yonder is a Lady vaild,
For properness beyond comparison,
And sure her face is like the rest: we'll see't.

GENTLEMAN
Why? you are hasty Sir already: know you
What 'tis you go about.

MARK-ANTONIO
Yes, I would see

The womans face.

GENTLEMAN
By heaven you shall not do't:
You do not know the custom of the place:
To draw that curtain here, though she were mean,
Is mortall.

MARK-ANTONIO
Is it? earth must come to earth
At last, and by my troth, I'll try it Sir.

GENTLEMAN
Then I must hold you fast. By all the faith
That can be plac'd in man, 'tis an attempt
More dangerous than death, 'tis death and shame:
I know the Lady well.

MARK-ANTONIO
Is she a Lady?
I shall the more desire to see her Sir.

GENTLEMAN
She is Alanso's wife, the Governor,
A noble Gentleman.

MARK-ANTONIO
Then let me go,
If I can win her, you and I will govern
This Town Sir, fear it not, and we will alter
These barbarous customs then; for every Lady
Shall be seen daily, and seen over too.

GENTLEMAN
Come, do not jest, nor let your passions bear you
To such wild enterprises: hold you still,
For as I have a soul, you shall not do't.
She is a Lady of unblemish'd fame,
And here to offer that affront, were base:
Hold on your way, and we will see the Town,
And overlook the Ladies.

MARK-ANTONIO
I am school'd,
And promise you I will: but good Sir, see,
She will pass by us now; I hope I may
Salute her thus far off.

GENTLEMAN
'S foot, are you mad?
'Twill be as ill as th' other.

1ST ATTENDANT
What's the matter?
What would that fellow have?

GENTLEMAN
Good Sir forbear.

1ST ATTENDANT
It seems you are new landed: would you beg
Any thing here?

MARK-ANTONIO
Yes Sir, all happiness
To that fair Lady, as I hope.

GENTLEMAN
Mark-antonio.

MARK-ANTONIO
Her face, which needs no hiding: I would beg
A sight of.

GENTLEMAN
Now go on, for 'tis too late
To keep this from a tumult.

1ST ATTENDANT
Sirrah, you
Shall see a fitter object for your eyes,
Then a fair Ladies face.

EUGENIA
For heavens sake, raise not
A quarrel in the streets for me.

1ST ATTENDANT
Slip in then;
This is your door.

EUGENIA
Will you needs quarrel then?

1ST ATTENDANT
We must, or suffer

This outrage: is't not all your minds Sirs, speak?

ALL
Yes.

EUGENIA
Then I do beseech ye, let my Lord

[Enter three or four **SOULDIERS**.

Not think the quarrel about me; for 'tis not.

[Exit.

GENTLEMAN
See happily some of our Galley souldiers
Are come ashoar.

1ST ATTENDANT
Come on Sir, you shall see
Faces enough.

GENTLEMAN
Some one of you call to

[Enter certain **TOWNSMEN**.

Our General, the whole rore of the Town
Comes in upon us.

MARK-ANTONIO
I have seen Sir better
Perhaps, than that was cover'd; and will yet
See that, or spoil yours.

[They fight.

[Enter **PHILIPPO**, **THEODOSIA** and **LEOCADIA**.

PHILIPPO
On, why start you back?

THEODOSIA
Alass Sir, they are fighting.

LEOCADIA
Let's be gone—

[**MARK-ANTONIO** falls.

See, see, a handsome man strook down.

GENTLEMAN
Ho General,
Look out, Antonio is in distress.

[Enter **RODORIGO** above.

THEODOSIA
Antonio.

LEOCADIA
Antonio! 'tis he.

RODRIGO [within]
Ho, Gunner make a shot into the Town,
I'll part you: bring away Antonio

[A shot fired off.

[Exeunt **ATTENDANTS** and **TOWNSMEN**.

Into my Cabben.

[Disappears from deck.

GENTLEMAN
I will do that office.
I fear it is the last, that I shall do him.

[Exit **SOULDIERS** and **GENTLEMEN** carrying **MARK-ANTONIO**.

THEODOSIA
The last, why will he dye?

[Faints.

LEOCADIA
Since I have found him: happiness leave me,
When I leave him.

[Exit.

PHILIPPO
Why Theodosia?
My sister; wake: alass, I griev'd but now

To see the streets so full; and now I grieve
To see them left so empty: I could wish,
Tumult himself were here, that yet at least
Amongst the band, I might espie some face
So pale and fearful, that would willingly
Embrace an arrand for a Cordial,
Or Aquavitæ, or a cup of sack,
Or a Physitian: but to talk of these
She breaths: stand up, O Theodosia,
Speak but as thou wert wont, give but a sigh,
Which is but the most unhappy piece of life,
And I will ever after worship sadness,
Apply my self to grief; prepare and build
Altars to sorrow.

THEODOSIA
O Philippo, help me.

PHILIPPO
I do; these are my arms, Philippo's arms,
Thy Brothers arms that hold thee up.

THEODOSIA
You help me
To life: but I would see Antonio
That's dead.

PHILIPPO
Thou shalt see any thing; how dost thou?

THEODOSIA
Better, I thank you.

PHILIPPO
Why that's well: call up
Thy senses, and uncloud thy cover'd spirits.
How now?

THEODOSIA
Recover'd: but Antonio,
Where is he?

PHILIPPO
We will find him: art thou well?

THEODOSIA
Perfectly well, saving the miss of him;
And I do charge you here, by our allyance,

And by the love which would have been betwixt us,
Knew we no kindred; by that killing fear,
Mingled with twenty thousand hopes and doubts,
Which you may think, plac'd in a Lovers heart,
And in a Virgins too, when she wants help,
To grant me your assistance, to find out
This man alive, or dead; and I will pay you
In service, tears, or prayers, a world of wealth:
But other treasure, I have none: alas!
You men have strong hearts; but we feeble maids
Have tender eyes, which only given be
To blind themselves, crying for what they see.

PHILIPPO
Why do'st thou charge me thus? have I been found
Slow to perform, what I could but imagine
Thy wishes were; have I at any time
Tender'd a business of mine own, beyond
A vanity of thine? have I not been
As if I were a sensless creature, made
To serve thee without pow'r of questioning,
If so, why fear'st thou?

THEODOSIA
I am satisfied.

PHILIPPO
Come; then let's go: where's Leocadia?

THEODOSIA
I know not Sir.

PHILIPPO
Where's Leocadia?

THEODOSIA
I do not know.

PHILIPPO
Leocadia,
This Tumult made the streets as dead as night,
A man may talk as freely: what's become
Of Leocadia?

THEODOSIA
She's run away.

PHILIPPO

Begone, and let us never more behold
Each others face, till we may, both together,
Fasten our eyes on her: accursed be
Those tender cozening names of charity,
And natural affection, they have lost
Me only by observing them, what cost
Travel, and fruitless wishes may in vain
Search through the world, but never find again.

THEODOSIA
Good Sir be patient, I have done no fault
Worthy this banishment.

PHILIPPO
Yes Leocadia,
The Lady so distress'd, who was content
To lay her story, and to lay her heart
As open as her story to your self,
Who was content, that I should know her Sex,
Before dissembl'd and to put her self
Into my conduct, whom I undertook
Safely to guard, is in this Tumult lost.

THEODOSIA
And can I help it Sir?

PHILIPPO
No, would thou couldst,
You might have done, but for that zeald religion
You women bear to swownings, you do pick
Your times to faint when some body is by:
Bound or by nature, or by love, or service
To raise you from that well dissembled death:
Inform me but of one that has been found
Dead in her private chamber by her self,
Where sickness would no more forbear, than here,
And I will quit the rest for her.

THEODOSIA
I know not
What they may do, and how they may dissemble;
But by my troth, I did not.

PHILIPPO
By my troth,
Would I had try'd; would I had let thee layn,
And followed her.

THEODOSIA
I would you had done so
Rather, than been so angry: where's Antonio?

PHILIPPO
Why do'st thou vex me with these questions?
I'll tell thee where, he's carried to the Galleys,
There to be chain'd, and row, and beat, and row
With knotted ropes, and pizzels; if he swound,
He has a dose of bisket.

THEODOSIA
I am glad
He is alive.

PHILIPPO
Was ever man thus troubled,
Tell me where Leocadia is?

THEODOSIA
Good brother be not so hasty, and I think I can:
You found no error in me, when I first
Told you she was a woman, and believe me
Something I have found out, which makes me think,
Nay, almost know so well, that I durst swear
She follow'd hurt Antonio.

PHILIPPO
What do we

[Enter the **GOVERNOR**, two **ATTENDANTS** and the **TOWNSMEN**.

Then lingring here; we will aboard the Galleys
And find her.

GOVERNOR
Made he a shot into the Town?

1ST ATTENDANT
He did Sir.

GOVERNOR
Call back those Gentlemen.

1ST ATTENDANT
The Governor, commands you back.

PHILIPPO

We will obey him Sir.

GOVERNOR
You gave him cause to shoot; I know, he is
So far from rash offence, and holds with me
Such curious friendship: could not one of you
Have call'd me while 'twas doing, such an uproar,
Before my dore too?

1ST TOWNSMAN
By my troth Sir, we were so busy in the publick cause, of our own
Private falling out: that we forgot it: at home we see now
You were not, but as soon as the shot made us fly, we ran
Away as fast as we could to seek your honor.

GOVERNOR
'Twas gravely done; but no man tells the cause
Or chance, or what it was that made you differ.

1ST TOWNSMAN
For my part Sir, if there were any that I knew
Of, the shot drove it out of my head, do you know any neighbours?

ALL
Not we, not we.

GOVERNOR
Not we! nor can you tell.

1ST ATTENDANT
No other cause,
But the old quarrel betwixt the Town and the Galleys.

GOVERNOR
Come nearer Gentlemen: what are your names?

PHILIPPO
My name Philippo.

THEODOSIA
And mine Theodoro.

GOVERNOR
Strangers you are it seems.

PHILIPPO
Newly arriv'd.

GOVERNOR
Then you are they begun this Tumult.

PHILIPPO
No Sir.

GOVERNOR
Speak one of you.

1ST ATTENDANT
They are not, I can quit 'em.

THEODOSIA
Yet we saw part, and an unhappy part
Of this debate, a long sought friend of ours
Strook down for dead, and born unto the Galleys,
His name is Mark-Antonio.

PHILIPPO
And another
Of our company, a Gentleman
Of noble birth, besides accompanyed
With all the gifts of nature, ravish'd hence
We know not how, in this dissention.

GOVERNOR
Get you home all, and work; and when I hear
You meddle with a weapon any more
But those belonging to your Trades, I'll lay you
Where your best Customers shall hardly find you.

[Exit **TOWNSMEN**.

I am sorry gentlemen, I troubled you,
Being both strangers, by your tongues, and looks,
Of worth: To make ye some part of amends
If there be any thing in this poor Town
Of Barcelona that you would command,
Command me.

THEODOSIA
Sir, this wounded Gentleman,
If it might please you, if your pow'r and love
Extend so far, I would be glad to wish
Might be remov'd into the Town for cure:
The Galleys stay not, and his wound I know
Cannot endure a voyage.

GOVERNOR
Sir, he shall,
I warrant you: Go call me hither Sirrah,
One of my other Servants.

[Exit **1ST ATTENDANT**.

PHILIPPO
And besides.
The Gentleman we lost, Signior Francisco,
Shall be render'd too.

[Enter a **SERVANT**.

GOVERNOR
And he Sir too: Go sirrah, bear this ring
To Roderigo, my most noble friend,
The General of the Galleys: Tell him this.

[Whispers to his **SERVANT**.

[Exit **SERVANT**.

THEODOSIA
Now we shall have 'em both.

PHILIPPO
Blest be thy thoughts
For apprehending this: blest be thy breath
For uttering it.

GOVERNOR
Come Gentlemen, you shall
Enter my roof: and I will send for Surgeons,
And you shall see your friends here presently.

THEODOSIA
His name was Mark-antonio.

GOVERNOR
I know it,
And have sent word so.

PHILIPPO
Did you not forget
Francisco's name?

GOVERNOR

Nor his: y'are truly welcome,
To talk about it more, were but to say
The same word often over: you are welcome.

[Exeunt.

Enter **MARK-ANTONIO**, carried, **LEOCADIA** following; and the **SERVANT**. **TWO SOULDIERS** carrying him.

SERVANT
This is the house Sir.

MARK-ANTONIO
Enter it, I pray you,
For I am faint, although I think my wound
Be nothing. Soldiers, leave us now: I thank you.

1ST SOULDIER
Heaven send you health Sir.

SERVANT
Let me lead you in.

MARK-ANTONIO
My wound's not in my feet; I shall entreat 'em
I hope to bear me so far.

[Exit with **LEOCADIA** and the **SERVANT**.

2ND SOULDIER
How seriously these land men fled, when our General made a
Shot, as if he had been a warning to call 'em to their Hall.

1ST SOULDIER
I cannot blame 'em, What man have they now in the
Town, able to maintain a Tumult, or uphold a matter out
Of square if need be? O the quiet hurley burleys that I
Have seen in this Town, when we have fought four hours
Together, and not a man amongst us so impertinent or
Modest to ask why? but now the pillars that bare
Up this blessed Town in that regular debate, and
Scambling, are dead, the more's the pitty.

2ND SOULDIER
Old Ignatio lives still.

1ˢᵀ SOULDIER
Yes, I know him: he will do prettily well at a mans liver:
But where is there any man now living in the Town
That hath a steady hand, and understands Anatomy
Well? if it come to a particular matter of the lungs,
Or the spleen, why? alas Ignatio is to seek; are
There any such men left as I have known, that
Would say they would hit you in this place? is there
Ever a good heartist, or a member-percer, or a
Small-gut man left in the Town, answer
Me that?

2ᴺᴰ SOULDIER
Mass, I think there be not.

1ˢᵀ SOULDIER
No, I warrant thee. Come, come, 'tis time
We were at the Galleys.

[Exeunt.

[Enter **GOVERNOR, EUGENIA, MARK-ANTONIO, PHILIPPO, THEODOSIA, LEOCADIA, ATTENDANTS.**

GOVERNOR
Sir, you may know by what I said already,
You may command my house; but I must beg
Pardon to leave you, if the publick business
Forc'd me not from you, I my self should call it
Unmannerly: but good Sir, do you give it
A milder name: it shall not be an hour
Ere I return.

MARK-ANTONIO
Sir, I was nere so poor
In my own thoughts, as that I want a means
To requite this with.

GOVERNOR
Sir, within this hour.

[Exit.

MARK-ANTONIO
This the Lady that I quarrell'd for?
O lust if wounds cannot restrain thy power,
Let shame: nor do I feel my hurt at all,
Nor is it ought, only I was well beaten:

If I pursue it, all the civil world
That ever did imagine the content
Found in the band of man and wife unbroke,
The reverence due to housholds, or the blemish
That may be stuck upon posterity
Will catch me, bind me, burn upon my forehead,
This is the wounded stranger, that receiv'd
For charity into a house, attempted—
I will not do it.

EUGENIA
Sir, how do you do now?
That you walk off.

MARK-ANTONIO
Worse Madam, than I was;
But it will over.

EUGENIA
Sit, and rest a while.

MARK-ANTONIO
Where are the Surgeons?

EUGENIA
Sir, it is their manner,
When they have seen the wound especially,
The patient being of worth, to go consult,
Which they are now at in another room,
About the dressing.

MARK-ANTONIO
Madam, I do feel my self not well.

THEODOSIA
Alass!

LEOCADIA
How do you Sir.

EUGENIA
Will you drink waters?

MARK-ANTONIO
No good Madam, 'tis not
So violent upon me; nor I think
Any thing dangerous: but yet there are
Some things that sit so heavy on my conscience,

That will perplex my mind, and stop my cure,
So that unless I utter 'em. A scratch
Here on my thumb will kill me: Gentlemen,
I pray you leave the room, and come not in
Your selves, or any other till I have
Open'd my self to this most honour'd Lady.

PHILIPPO
We will not.

THEODOSIA
O blest! he will discover now
His love to me.

LEOCADIA
Now he will tell the Lady
Our Contract.

[Exit.

EUGENIA
I do believe he will confess to me
The wrong he did a Lady in the streets;
But I forgive him.

MARK-ANTONIO
Madam, I perceive
My self grow worse and worse.

EUGENIA
Shall I call back your friends?

MARK-ANTONIO
O no, but e'r I do impart
What burthens me so sore, let me intreat you,
(For there is no trust in these Surgeons)
To look upon my wound; it is perhaps
My last request: But tell me truely too,
That must be in: how far do you imagine
It will have pow'r upon me.

EUGENIA
Sir, I will.

MARK-ANTONIO
For heavens sake, softly: oh, I must needs lay
My head down easily, whilst you do it.

EUGENIA
Do Sir,
'Tis but an ordinary blow; a child
Of mine has had a greater, and been well;
Are you faint hearted?

MARK-ANTONIO
Oh.

EUGENIA
Why do you sigh?
There is no danger in the world in this;
I wonder it should make a man sit down;
What do you mean, why do you kiss my breasts?
Lift up your head, your wound, may well endure it.

MARK-ANTONIO
O Madam, may I not express affection,
Dying-affection too I fear, to those
That do me favors, such as this of yours.

EUGENIA
If you mean so, 'tis well; but what's the business
Lies on your conscience?

MARK-ANTONIO
I will tell you Madam.

EUGENIA
Tell me and laugh?

MARK-ANTONIO
But I will tell you true
Though I do laugh, I know as well as you
My wound is nothing, nor the power of earth
Could lay a wound upon me in your presence,
That I could feel; but I do laugh to think
How covertly, how far beyond the reach
Of men, and wise men too, we shall deceive 'em,
Whilst they imagine I am talking here
With that short breath I have, ready to swound
At every full point; you my ghostly Mother
To hear my sad confession, you and I
Will on that bed within, prepar'd for me,
Debate the matter privately.

EUGENIA
Forbear,

Thou wert but now as welcome to this house
As certain cures to sick men, and just now
This sudain alteration makes thee look
Like plagues come to infect it; if thou knewst
How loathsome thou wilt be, thou wouldst intreat
These wals, or posts to help thee to a hurt,
Past thy dissimulation.

MARK-ANTONIO
Gentle Madam
Call 'em not in?

EUGENIA
I will not yet, this place
I know to be within the reach of tongue,
And ears, thou canst not force me; therefore hear me
What I will tell thee quickly, thou art born
To end some way more disesteem'd than this,
Or which is worse, to dye of this hurt yet.
Come Gentlemen.

[Enter **LEOCADIA**.

MARK-ANTONIO
Good Madam.

EUGENIA
Gentlemen.

LEOCADIA
Madam how is't? is Mark-antonio well?
Methinks your looks are alter'd, and I see
A strange distemper in you.

EUGENIA
I am wrought
By that dissembling man, that fellow worth
Nothing but kicking.

[Enter **PHILIPPO** and **THEODOSIA**.

LEOCADIA
Gentle Madam speak
To me alone let not them understand
His fault, he will repent it I dare swear.

EUGENIA
I'll tell it you in private.

PHILIPPO
Mark-antonio,
How do you?

MARK-ANTONIO
Stand farther off I pray you
Give me some ayre.

THEODOSIA
Good Brother, will he scape,
The Surgeons say there is no danger.

PHILIPPO
Scape?
No doubt he will.

LEOCADIA
Alas will he not leave
This trying all; Madam, I do beseech you
Let me but speak to him, you and these by,
And I dare almost promise you to make him
Shew himself truly sorrowful to you,
Besides a story I shall open to you,
Not put in so good words but in it self
So full of chance, that you will easily
Forgive my tediousness, and be well pleas'd
With that so much afflicts me.

EUGENIA
Good Sir do.

LEOCADIA
And I desire no interruption
Of speech may trouble me till I have said
What I will quickly do.

THEODOSIA
What will she say.

EUGENIA
Come Gentlemen, I pray you lend your ears,
And keep your voyces.

LEOCADIA
Signior Mark-antonio
How do you do?

MARK-ANTONIO
Oh the Surgeons.

LEOCADIA
Let me tell you
Who know as well as you, you do dissemble,
It is no time to do so; leave the thoughts
Of this vain world, forget your flesh and blood,
And make your spirit an untroubled way
To pass to what it ought.

MARK-ANTONIO
Y're not in earnest?
Why I can walk Sir, and am well.

LEOCADIA
'Tis true
That you can walk, and do believe y're well:
It is the nature, as your Surgeons say
Of these wounds, for a man to go, and talk,
Nay merrily, till his last hour, his minute:
For heaven sake Sir, sit down again.

MARK-ANTONIO
Alass
Where are the Surgeons?

LEOCADIA
Sir, they will not come,
If they should dress you, you would dye they say
Ere one would tell twenty; trouble not your mind,
Keep your head warm, and do not stir your body,
And you may live an hour.

MARK-ANTONIO
Oh heavens, an hour?
Alass, it is too little to remember
But half the wrongs that I have done; how short
Then for contrition, and how least of all
For satisfaction?

LEOCADIA
But you desire
To satisfie?

MARK-ANTONIO
Heaven knows I do.

LEOCADIA

Then know
That I am he, or she, or what you will
Most wrong'd by you; your Leocadia,
I know you must remember me.

MARK-ANTONIO

Oh heaven!

LEOCADIA

That lost her friends, that lost her fathers house,
That lost her fame in loosing of her Sex,
With these strange garments, there is no excuse
To hinder me, it is within your power
To give me satisfaction; you have time
Left in this little piece of life to do it:
Therefore I charge you for your conscience sake,
And for our fame, which I would fain have live
When both of us are dead, to celebrate
That Contract; which you have both seal'd and sworn
Yet ere you dye, which must be hastily
Heaven knows.

MARK-ANTONIO

Alass, the sting of conscience
To death-ward for our faults; draw nearer all
And hear what I unhappy man shall say;
First Madam I desire your pardon; next
(I feel my spirits fail me) Gentlemen
Let me shake hands with you, and let's be friends,
For I have done wrong upon wrong so thick
I know not where, that every man methinks
Should be mine enemy; Forgive me both.
Lastly 'tis true (oh I do feel the power
Of death seize on me) that I was contracted
By seal and oath to Leocadia;
(I must speak fast, because I fear my life
Will else be shorter than my speech would be)
But 'tis impossible to satisfie
You Leocadia, but by repentance,
Though I can dyingly, and boldly say
I know not your dishonor, yet that was
Your virtue, and not mine, you know it well;
But herein lies th' impossibility,
O Theodosia, Theodosia
I was betroth'd to Theodosia
Before I ever saw thee; heaven forgive me
She is my wife this half hour whilst I live.

THEODOSIA
That's I, that's I, I'm Theodosia,
Hear me a little now, who have not suffer'd
Disgrace at all methinks, since you confess
What I so long have sought for, here is with me
Philippo too my Brother.

MARK-ANTONIO
I am glad;
All happiness to him; come let me kiss thee
Beg pardon of that Maid for my offence,
And let me farther, with a dying breath
Tell in thine ear the rest of my desires.

EUGENIA
I am afraid they will all four turn women
If we hold longer talk.

LEOCADIA
Alass there is
No hope for me; that's Theodosia
And that her Brother, I am only sorry
I was beholding to 'em; I will search
Over the world, as careless of my fortunes,
As they of me, till I can meet a curse
To make these almost killing-sorrows worse.

[Exit.

THEODOSIA
Sir, as I live she ly'd, only to draw
A just confession from you, which she hath
A happy one for me, ask of this Lady,
Ask of my Brother.

EUGENIA
Sir, she did dissemble,
Your wound is nothing.

PHILIPPO
Leocadia's gone.

[Exit.

THEODOSIA
Rise up, and stir your self, 'tis but amazement
And your imagination that afflicts you,

Look you Sir now.

MARK-ANTONIO
I think 'tis so indeed.

THEODOSIA
The Surgeons do not come, because they swear
It needs no dressing.

EUGENIA
You shall talk with 'em
Within, for your own fancy.

MARK-ANTONIO
Where's your Brother, and Leocadia?

EUGENIA
Within belike.

MARK-ANTONIO
I feel my self methinks as well as ever.

EUGENIA
Keep then your mind so too; I do forgive
The fault you did to me; But here is one
Must not be wrong'd hereafter.

MARK-ANTONIO
Neither shall she
When I make jests of oaths again, or make
My lust play with religion, when I leave
To keep true joys for her, and yet within
My self true sorrow for my passed deeds
May I want grace, when I would fain repent,
And find a great and sodain punishment.

[Exeunt.

ACTUS QUINTUS

SCÆNA PRIMA

Barcelona. A Street.

Enter **PHILIPPO**, **DIEGO**, and **INCUBO**.

PHILIPPO
Where is mine Host, did not he see him neither?

DIEGO
Not I, i'faith Sir.

PHILIPPO
Nor the muleter?

INCUBO
Nay he is past seeing, unless it be in's sleep,
By this time; all his visions were the pots,
Three hours since Sir.

PHILIPPO
Which way should she take?
Nay, look you now; do you all stand still? good Heaven
You might have lighted on him, now this instant?
For loves sake seek him out, who ever find him
I will reward his fortune as his diligence;
Get all the Town to help, that will be hir'd,
Their pains I'll turn to annual holiday,
If it shall chance, but one bring word of her,
Pray you about it.

INCUBO
Her Sir? who do you mean?

PHILIPPO
(I had forgot my self) the Page I meant
That came along with us.

DIEGO
He you gave the clothes too?

PHILIPPO
I ga' the clothes to; Rascal?

DIEGO
Nay good Sir.

PHILIPPO
Why dost thou mention or upbraid my courtesies
Slave?

DIEGO
For your honor Sir.

PHILIPPO
Wretch; I was honor'd,
That she would wear 'em (he, I would say) 's death?
Go, get, and find 'em out, or never see me,
I shall betray my love e'r I possess it,
Some Star direct me, or ill Planet strike me.

[Exit **PHILIPPO**.

INCUBO
Best to divide.

DIEGO
I'll this way.

INCUBO
And I this.

DIEGO
I, as you, find him for a Real.

INCUBO
'Tis done.

DIEGO
My course is now directly to some Pie-house
I know the Pages compass.

INCUBO
I think rather
The smock-side o'th' Town, the surer harbor
At his years to put in.

DIEGO
If I do find
The hungry haunt, I take him by the teeth now.

INCUBO
I by the tail, yet I as you.

DIEGO
No more.

[Exeunt.

SCÆNA SECUNDA

Another Street.

Enter **PHILIPPO**.

PHILIPPO
Dear Leocadia, where canst thou be fled
Thus like a spirit hence? and in a moment?
What cloud can hide thee from my following search
If yet thou art a body? sure she hath not
Tane any house? she did too late leave one
Where all humanity of a place receiv'd her,
And would, (if she had staid) have help'd to right
The wrong her fortune did her; yet she must
Be inter'd somewhere, or be found, no street,
Lane, passage, corner, turn, hath scap'd enquiry:
If her despair had ravish'd her to air
She could not yet be ratified so
But some of us should meet her? though their eyes
Perhaps be leaden, and might turn; mine would
Strike out a lightning for her, and divide
A mist as thick as ever darkness was,
Nay see her through a quarry; they do lye,
Lye grosly that say love is blind; by him,
And heaven they lye; he has a sight can pierce
Through Ivory, as cleer as it were horn,
And reach his object.

[Enter **INCUBO**.

INCUBO
Sir, he's found, he's found.

PHILIPPO
Ha? where? But reach that happy Note again
And let it relish truth, thou art an Angel.

INCUBO
He's here; fast by Sir, calling for a Boat
To go aboard the Gallies.

PHILIPPO
Where, where; hold thee.

[Exit.

INCUBO
He might ha' kept this now, I had nought to shew for't,

If he had had the wit t' have gone from's word,
These direct men, they are no men of fashion,
Talk what you will, this is a very smelt.

[Exit.

SCÆNA TERTIA

A Room in the house of the Surgeon.

Enter **LEONARDO** with a **SURGEON**.

LEONARDO
Upon your Art Sir, and your faith to assist it
Shall I believe you then his wound's not mortal?

SURGEON
Sir, 'tis not worth your question; less your fear.

LEONARDO
You doe restore me Sir, I pray you accept
This small remembrance of a fathers thanks
For so assur'd a benefit.

SURGEON
Excuse me.

LEONARDO
Sir, I can spare it, and must not believe
But that your fortune may receiv't, except
You'ld ha' me think you live not by your practice.

SURGEON
I crave your pardon Sir; you teach me manners.

LEONARDO
I crave your love and friendship, and require
As I have made now, both my self and business
A portion of your care, you will but bring me
Under the person of a call'd assistant
To his next opening, where I may but see him,
And utter a few words to him in private,
And you will merit me; for I am loth
Since here I have not to appear my self,
Or to be known unto the Governor,
Or make a tumult of my purpose.

SURGEON
Neither
I hope will be your need Sir; I shall bring you
Both there, and off again without the hazard.

[Exeunt.

The Harbour.

Enter **PHILIPPO** and **LEOCADIA**.

PHILIPPO
Will you not hear me!

LEOCADIA
I have heard so much
Will keep me deaf for ever; No, Mark-antonio
After thy sentence, I may hear no more,
Thou hast pronounc'd me dead.

PHILIPPO
Appeal to reason,
She will reprieve you from the power of grief,
Which rules but in her absence; Hear me say
A soveraign message from her, which in duty,
And love to your own safety, you ought hear:
Why do you strive so? whither would you flie?
You cannot wrest your self away from care
You may from counsel; you may shift your place
But not your person; and another Clyme
Makes you no other.

LEOCADIA
Oh.

PHILIPPO
For passions sake,
(Which I do serve, honor, and love in you)
If you will sigh, sigh here; If you would vary
A sigh to tears, or out-cry, do it here.
No shade, no desart, darkness, nor the grave
Shall be more equal to your thoughts than I,
Only but hear me speak.

LEOCADIA
What would you say?

PHILIPPO
That which shall raise your heart, or pull down mine,
Quiet your passion, or provoke mine own;
We must have both one balsome, or one wound,
For know (lov'd fair) since the first providence
Made me your rescue, I have read you through,
And with a wondring pity look'd on you,
I have observ'd the method of your blood,
And waited on it even with sympathy
Of a like Red, and Paleness in mine own;
I knew which blush was angers, which was loves,
Which was the eye of sorrow, which of truth:
And could distinguish honor from disdain
In every change: and you are worth my study;
I saw your voluntary misery
Sustain'd in travel: A disguis'd Maid
Wearied with seeking: and with finding lost,
Neglected, where you hop'd most, or put by;
I saw it, and have laid it to my heart,
And though it were my Sister which was righted,
Yet being by your wrong, I put off nature,
Could not be glad, where I was bound to triumph;
My care for you, so drown'd respect of her;
Nor did I only apprehend your bonds,
But studied your release: and for that day
Have I made up a ransom, brought you health
Preservative 'gainst chance, or injury
Please you apply it to the grief; my self.

LEOCADIA
Humph.

PHILIPPO
Nay, do not think me less than such a cure,
Antonio was not; And 'tis possible
Philippo may succeed: My bloud and house
Are as deep rooted: and as fairly spread,
As Mark-antonio's, and in that, all seek,
Fortune hath given him no precedency:
As for our thanks to Nature I may burn
Incense as much as he; I ever durst
Walk with Antonio by the self-same light
At any feast, or triumph, and ne'r car'd
Which side my Lady or her woman took

In their survey; I durst have told my tale too
Though his discourse new ended.

LEOCADIA
My repulse.

PHILIPPO
Let not that torture you, which makes me happy
Nor think that conscience (fair) which is no shame
'Twas no repulse, I was your Dowry rather:
For then methought a thousand graces met
To make you lovely, and ten thousand stories
Of constant virtue, which you then out-reach'd,
In one example did proclaim you rich:
Nor do I think you wretched, or disgrac'd,
After this suffering, and do therefore take
Advantage of your need; but rather know
You are the charge and business of those powers,
Who, like best Tutors, do inflict hard tasks
Upon great Natures, and of noblest hopes;
Read trivial Lessons, and halfe lines to sluggs;
They that live long, and never feel mischance,
Spend more than halfe their age in ignorance.

LEOCADIA
'Tis well you think so.

PHILIPPO
You shall think so too,
You shall sweet Leocadia, and do so.

LEOCADIA
Good Sir no more; you have too fair a shape
To play so foul a part in, as the Tempter:
Say that I could make peace with fortune, who,
Who should absolve me of my vow yet; ha?
My Contract made?

PHILIPPO
Your Contract?

LEOCADIA
Yes, my Contract,
Am I not his? his wife?

PHILIPPO
Sweet, nothing less.

LEOCADIA

I have no name then?

PHILIPPO

Truly then you have not;
How can you be his wife, who was before
Anothers Husband?

LEOCADIA

Oh, though he dispence
With his faith given, I cannot with mine.

PHILIPPO

You do mistake (cleer soul) his precontract
Doth annul yours, and you have giv'n no faith
That ties you in Religion, or humanity,
You rather sin against that greater precept,
To covet what's anothers; Sweet, you do
Believe me, who dare not urge dishonest things,
Remove that scruple therefore, and but take
Your dangers now, into your judgements skale
And weigh them with your safeties: Think but whither
Now you can goe: what you can do to live?
How near you ha' barr'd all Ports to your own succor,
Except this one that I here open: Love
Should you be left alone, you were a prey
To the wild lust of any, who would look
Upon this shape like a temptation
And think you want the man you personate
Would not regard this shift, which love put on
As virtue forc'd, but covet it like vice;
So should you live the slander of each Sex,
And be the child of error and of shame,
And which is worse, even Mark-antonie
Would be call'd just, to turn a wanderer off,
And Fame report you worthy his contempt;
Where if you make new choice, and settle here
There is no further tumult in this flood,
Each current keeps his course, and all suspitions
Shall return honors: Came you forth a Maid?
Go home a Wife? alone? and in disguise?
Go home a waited Leocadia:
Go home, and by the virtue of that charm
Transform all mischiefs, as you are transform'd;
Turn your offended Fathers wrath to wonder,
And all his loud grief to a silent welcome:
Unfold the Riddles you have made, what say you?
Now is the time; delay is but despair,

If you be chang'd, let a kiss tell me so.

LEOCADIA
I am: but how, I rather feel than know.

[He kisses her.

[Enter **SANCHIO** carried, **ALPHONSO** and **SERVANTS**.

SANCHIO
Come Sir; you are welcome now to Barcelona,
Take off my hood.

PHILIPPO
Who be these? stay, let's view 'em?

ALPHONSO
'Twas a long journey: are you not weary Sir?

SANCHO
Weary? I could have rid it in mine Armour.

LEOCADIA
Alas!

PHILIPPO
What ail you dear?

LEOCADIA
It is my Father.

PHILIPPO
Your Father: which?

LEOCADIA
He that is carried: oh
Let us make hence.

PHILIPPO
For loves sake: good my heart.

LEOCADIA
Into some house before he see me.

PHILIPPO
Dear,
Be not thus frighted.

LEOCADIA
Oh his wrath is tempest.

PHILIPPO
Sweet, take your spirit to you, and stay, be't he,
He cannot know you in this habit, and me
I'm sure he less knows, for he never saw me.

ALPHONSO
Ha? who is that? my Son Philippo?

PHILIPPO
Sir.

ALPHONSO
Why, what make you here? Is this Salamanca?
And that your study? ha? nay stay him too,
We'll see him by his leave.

SERVANT
You must not strive Sir.

ALPHONSO
No, no, come near.

SANCHIO
My Daughter: Leocadia?

ALPHONSO
How Sir, your Daughter?

SANCHIO
Yes Sir, and as sure
As that's your Son: Come hither: what now? run
Out o' your sex? breech'd? was't not enough
At once to leave thy Father, and thine honor,
Unless th' hadst quit thy self too.

PHILIPPO
Sir, what fault
She can be urg'd of, I must take on me
The guilt and punishment.

SANCHIO
You must Sir: how
If you shall not, though you must? I deal not
With boys Sir; I, you have a Father here
Shall do me right.

ALPHONSO
Thou art not mad Philippo?
Art thou Mark-antonie? Son to Leonardo?
Our business is to them.

SANCHIO
No, no, no, no.

[**LEOCADIA** steals out.

I'll ha' the business now; with you, none else,
Pray you let's speak, in private: (carry me to him)
Your Son's the ravisher Sir, and here I find him:
I hope you'll give me cause to think you noble,
And do me right, with your sword Sir, as becomes
One gentleman of honor to another;
All this is fair Sir: here's the Sea fast by,
Upon the sands, we will determine
'Tis that I call you to; let's make no daies on't,
I'll lead your way; to the sea-side Rascals.

PHILIPPO
Sir
I would beseech your stay; he may not follow you.

SANCHIO
No, turn, I'll kill him here then: Slaves, Rogues, Bloks.
Why do you not bear me to him? ha' you been
Acquainted with my motions, loggs, so long
And yet not know to time 'em.

PHILIPPO
Were you Sir
Not impotent.

ALPHONSO
Hold you your peace Boy.

SANCHIO
Impotent,
'Death, I'll cut his throat first, and then his Fathers.

ALPHONSO
You must provide you then a sharper Razor
Than is your tongue, for I not fear your sword.

SANCHIO

'Heart bear me to either of 'em.

PHILIPPO
Pray Sir your patience.

[Enter **GOVERNOR** and **ATTENDANTS**.

ALPHONSO
My curse light on thee if thou stay him.

PHILIPPO
Hold.

GOVERNOR
Why, what's the matter, Gentlemen, what tumult
Is this you raise i'th' street? before my door?
Know you what 'tis to draw a weapon here?

SANCHIO
Yes, and to use it (bear me up to him, Rogues)
Thus, at a Traitors heart.

ALPHONSO
Truer than thine.

GOVERNOR
Strike, strike; Some of the people disarm 'em,
Kill 'em if they resist.

PHILIPPO
Nay generous Sir
Let not your courtesie turn fury now.

GOVERNOR
Lay hold upon 'em, take away their weapons,
I will be worth an answer, e'r we part.

PHILIPPO
'Tis the Governor Sir.

ALPHONSO
I yield my self.

SANCHIO
My Sword? what thinkst thou of me? pray thee tell me.

1ST ATTENTDANT
As of a Gentleman.

SANCHIO
No more?

1ˢᵀ ATTENDANT
Of worth,
And quality.

SANCHIO
And I should quit my sword
There were small worth or quality in that friend;
Pray thee learn thou more worth and quality
Than to demand it.

GOVERNOR
Force it I say.

1ˢᵀ ATTENDANT
The Governor
You hear, commands.

SANCHIO
The Governr shall pardon me.

PHILIPPO
How, Leocadia gone again?

[Exit **PHILIPPO**.

SANCHIO
He shall friend
I' th' point of honor; by his leave, so tell him,
His person and authority I acknowledge,
And do submit me to it; but my Sword,
He shall excuse me, were he fifteen Governors;
That and I dwell together, and must yet
Till my hands part, assure him.

GOVERNOR
I say force it.

[His sword is taken from him.

SANCHIO
Stay, hear me. Hast thou ever read Caranza?
Understandst thou honor, Noble Governor?

GOVERNOR

For that we'll have more fit dispute.

SANCHIO
Your name Sir?

GOVERNOR
You shall know that too: but on colder terms,
Your blood and brain are now too hot to take it.

SANCHIO
Force my Sword from me? this is an affront.

GOVERNOR
Bring 'em away.

SANCHIO
You'll do me reparation.

[Exeunt.

[Enter **PHILIPPO**.

PHILIPPO
I have for ever lost her, and am lost,
And worthily: my lameness hath undone me;
She's gone hence, asham'd of me: yet I seek her.
Will she be ever found to me again,
Whom she saw stand so poorly, and dare nothing
In her defence, here? when I should have drawn
This Sword out like a Meteor, and have shot it
In both our Parents eies, and left 'em blind
Unto their impotent angers? Oh I am worthy
On whom this loss and scorn should light to death
Without the pity that should wish me better,
Either alive, or in my Epitaph.

[Exit.

SCÆNA QUINTA

[Enter **LEONARDO, MARK-ANTONIO**.

LEONARDO
Well Son, your Father is too near himself
And hath too much of nature to put off
Any affection that belongs to you,

I could have only wish'd you had acquainted
Her Father, whom it equally concerns,
Though y'had presum'd on me: it might have open'd
An easier gate, and path to both our joyes:
For though I am none of those flinty Fathers
That when their children do but natural things,
Turn rock and offence straight: yet Mark-antonio,
All are not of my quarry.

MARK-ANTONIO
'Tis my fear Sir;
And if hereafter I should e'r abuse
So great a piety, it were my malice.

[Enter **ATTENDANTS**.

ATTENDANT
We must intreat you Gentlemen to take
Another room, the Governor is coming
Here, on some business.

[Enter **GOVERNOR, SANCHIO, ALPHONSO, ATTENDANTS**.

MARK-ANTONIO
We will give him way.

SANCHIO
I will have right Sir on you; that believe,
If there be any Marshals Court in Spain.

GOVERNOR
For that Sir we shall talk.

SANCHIO
—Do not slight me,
Though I am without a Sword.

GOVERNOR
Keep to your Chair Sir.

SANCHIO
—Let me fall, and hurle my chair! slaves at him!

GOVERNOR
You are the more temper'd man Sir: let me intreat
Of you the manner how this brawl fell out.

ALPHONSO

Fell out? I know not how: nor do I care much:
But here we came Sir to this Town together,
Both in one business, and one wrong, engag'd,
To seek one Leonardo, an old Genoese,
I ha' said enough there; would you more? false father
Of a false son, call'd Mark-antonio,
Who had stole both our Daughters; and which Father
Conspiring with his Son in treachery,
It seem'd, to flie our satisfaction,
Was, as we heard, come private to this Town
Here to take ship for Italy.

[Re-Enter **LEONARDO** and **MARK-ANTONIO**.

LEONARDO
You heard
More than was true then: by the fear, or falshood,
And though I thought not to reveal my self
(Pardon my manners in't to you) for some
Important reasons; yet being thus character'd
And challeng'd, know I dare appear, and doe
To who dares threaten.

MARK-ANTONIO
I say he is not worthy
The name of man, or any honest preface,
That dares report or credit such a slander.
Do you Sir say it?

ALPHONSO
I doe say it.

GOVERNOR
Hold.
Is this your father Signior Mark-antonio?
You have ill requited me thus to conceal him
From him would honor him, and do him service.

[Enter **EUGENIA**.

LEONARDO
'Twas not his fault Sir.

EUGENIA
Where's my Lord?

GOVERNOR
Sweet-heart.

EUGENIA
Know you these Gentlemen? they are all the fathers
Unto our friends.

GOVERNOR
So it appears my Dove.

SANCHIO
Sir, I say nothing: I do want a Sword.
And till I have a Sword I will say nothing.

EUGENIA
Good Sir, command these Gentlemen their Arms;
Entreat 'em as your friends, not as your prisoners.
Where be their Swords?

[**ATTENDANTS** restore their swords to **SANCHIO** and **ALPHONSO**.

GOVERNOR
Restore each man his weapon.

SANCHIO
It seems thou hast not read Caranza, fellow
I must have reparation of honor,
As well as this: I find that wounded.

GOVERNOR
Sir,
I did not know your quality, if I had
'Tis like I should have done you more respects.

SANCHIO
It is sufficient, by Caranza's rule.

EUGENIA
I know it is Sir.

SANCHIO
Have you read Caranza Lady?

EUGENIA
If you mean him that writ upon the Duel,
He was my kinsman.

SANCHIO
Lady, then you know
By the right noble writings of your kinsman,

My honor is as dear to me, as the Kings.

EUGENIA
'Tis very true Sir.

SANCHIO
Therefore I must crave
Leave to go on now with my first dependance.

EUGENIA
What ha' you more?

GOVERNOR
None here good Signior.

SANCHIO
I will, refer me to Caranza still.

EUGENIA
Nay love, I prethee let me manage this.
With whom is't Sir?

SANCHIO
With that false man Alphonso.

EUGENIA
Why he has th' advantage Sir, in legs.

SANCHIO
But I
In truth, in hand and heart, and a good Sword.

EUGENIA
But how if he will not stand you Sir?

ALPHONSO
For that,
Make it no question Lady, I will stick
My feet in earth down by him, where he dare.

SANCHIO
O would thou wouldst.

ALPHONSO
I'll do't.

SANCHIO
Let me kiss him.

I fear thou wilt not yet.

EUGENIA
Why Gentlemen,
If you'll proceed according to Caranza,
Methinks an easier way, were two good chairs,
So you would be content Sir, to be bound,
'Cause he is lame? I'll fit you with like weapons,
Pistols and Ponyards, and ev'n end it. If
The difference between you be so mortal,
It cannot be tane up.

SANCHIO
Tane up? take off
This head first.

ALPHONSO
Come bind me in a chair.

EUGENIA
Yes, do.

GOVERNOR
What mean you, Dove.

EUGENIA
Let me alone,
And set 'em at their distance: when you ha' done
Lend me two Ponyards; I'll have Pistols ready
Quickly.

[Exit.

[Enter **PHILIPPO**.

PHILIPPO
She is not here Mark-antonio,
Saw you not Leocadia?

MARK-ANTONIO
Not I brother.

PHILIPPO
Brother let's speak with you; you were false unto her.

MARK-ANTONIO
I was, but have ask'd pardon: why do you urge it?

PHILIPPO
You were not worthy of her.

MARK-ANTONIO
May be I was not;
But 'tis not well, you tell me so.

PHILIPPO
My Sister
Is not so fair.

MARK-ANTONIO
It skils not.

PHILIPPO
Nor so virtuous.

MARK-ANTONIO
Yes, she must be as virtuous.

PHILIPPO
I would fain—

MARK-ANTONIO
What brother?

PHILIPPO
Strike you.

MARK-ANTONIO
I shall not bear strokes,
Though I do these strange words.

PHILIPPO
Will you not kill me?

MARK-ANTONIO
For what good brother?

PHILIPPO
Why, for speaking well
Of Leocadia.

MARK-ANTONIO
No indeed.

PHILIPPO
Nor ill

Of Theodosia?

[Enter **EUGENIA**, **LEOCADIA**, **THEODOSIA**, and one with two Pistols.

MARK-ANTONIO
Neither.

PHILIPPO
Fare you well then.

EUGENIA
Nay, you shall have as noble seconds too
As ever Duelists had; give 'em their weapons:

[**SANCHIO** and **ALPHONSO** receive the weapons.

Now St. Jago!

SANCHIO
Are they charg'd?

EUGENIA
Charg'd Sir?
I warrant you.

ALPHONSO
Would they were well discharg'd.

SANCHIO
I like a Sword much better I confess.

EUGENIA
Nay, wherefore stay you? shall I mend your mark?
Strike one another, thorough these?

PHILIPPO
My love.

ALPHONSO
My Theodosia.

SANCHIO
I ha' not the heart.

ALPHONSO
Nor I.

EUGENIA

Why here is a dependence ended.
Unbind that Gentleman; come take here to you
Your Sons and Daughters, and be friends. A feast
Waits you within, is better than your fray:
Lovers, take you your own, and all forbear
Under my roof, either to blush or fear.
My love, what say you? could Caranza himself
Carry a business better?

GOVERNOR
It is well:
All are content I hope, and we well eas'd.
If they for whom we have done all this be pleas'd.

[Exeunt.

Francis Beaumont – A Short Biography

Francis Beaumont was born in 1584 near the small Leicestershire village of Thringstone. Unfortunately precise records of much of his short life do not exist.

He was the son to Sir Francis Beaumont of Grace Dieu, a justice of the common pleas. His mother was Anne, the daughter of Sir George Pierrepont.

The first date we can give for his education is at age 13 when he begins at Broadgates Hall (now Pembroke College, Oxford). Sadly, his father died the following year, 1598. Beaumont left university without a degree and entered the Inner Temple in London in 1600. A career choice of Law taken previously by his father.

The information to hand is confident that Beaumont's career in law was short-lived. He was quickly attracted to the theatre and soon became first an admirer and then a student of poet and playwright Ben Jonson. Jonson at this time was a cultural behemoth; very talented and a life full of volatility that included frequent brushes with the authorities. His followers, including the poet Robert Herrick, were known as 'the sons of Ben'. Beaumont was also on friendly terms with other luminaries such as the poet Michael Drayton.

Beaumont's first work was Salmacis and Hermaphroditus, it debuted in 1602. A 1911 edition of the Encyclopædia Britannica includes the description "not on the whole discreditable to a lad of eighteen, fresh from the popular love-poems of Marlowe and Shakespeare, which it naturally exceeds in long-winded and fantastic diffusion of episodes and conceits."

By 1605, Beaumont had written commendatory verses to Volpone one of Ben Jonson's masterpieces.

It was now, in the early years of the 17th Century, that he met John Fletcher and together they gradually formed one of the most dynamic and productive of writing teams that English theatre has ever produced.

Their playwriting careers at this stage were both troubled by early failure. Beaumont had written The Knight of the Burning Pestle and it was first performed by the Children of the Blackfriars company in 1607. The audience however was distinctly unimpressed. The publisher's epistle in the 1613 quarto says they failed to note "the privie mark of irony about it."

The following year, Fletcher's Faithful Shepherdess failed on the same stage.

In 1609, however, the two collaborated in earnest on Philaster. The play was performed by the King's Men at the Globe Theatre and at Blackfriars. It was a great success. Their careers were now well and truly launched and into the bargain they had ignited and captured a public taste for tragicomedy.

There is an account that at the time the two men shared everything. They lived together in a house on the Bankside in Southwark, " they also lived together in Bankside, sharing clothes and having "one wench in the house between them." Or as another account puts it "sharing everything in the closest intimacy."

This arrangement stopped in about 1613 when Beaumont married Ursula Isley, daughter and co-heiress of Henry Isley of Sundridge in Kent, by whom he had two daughters (one of them was born after his death).

Beaumont, at a very young age even for those times, was struck down by a stroke at some point in mid-1613, after which he was unable to write any more plays, but he did manage to write an elegy for Lady Penelope Clifton, who had died on 26th October 1613.

Francis Beaumont died on March 6th, 1616 and was buried in Westminster Abbey.

In his short life his canon was small but influential. Although he is seen more as a dramatist his poetry was celebrated even then and it continues to gain an avid readership to this day.

It was said at one point of the collaboration of Beaumont and Fletcher that "in their joint plays their talents are so ... completely merged into one, that the hand of Beaumont cannot clearly be distinguished from that of Fletcher." Whilst it was the view then it has not endured into modern times. Indeed, slowly but with certainty the name of Beaumont has been removed from many of their joint works. It has given way to other such luminaries as Philip Massinger, Nathan field and James Shirley.

John Fletcher – A Short Biography

John Fletcher was born in December, 1579 in Rye, Sussex. He was baptised on December 20th.

As can be imagined details of much of his life and career have not survived and, accordingly, only a very brief indication of his life and works can be given.

His father, Richard Fletcher, was a successful and rather ambitious cleric. From being the Dean of Peterborough he moved on to become the Bishop of Bristol, Bishop of Worcester and finally, shortly before his death, the Bishop of London. He was also the chaplain to Queen Elizabeth.

When he was Dean of Peterborough, Richard Fletcher, witnessed the execution of Mary, Queen of Scots. It was said he "knelt down on the scaffold steps and started to pray out loud and at length, in a prolonged and rhetorical style, as though determined to force his way into the pages of history". He cried out at her death, "So perish all the Queen's enemies!" All very dramatic but the family did have strong links to the Arts.

Young Fletcher appears at the very young age of eleven to have entered Corpus Christi College at Cambridge University in 1591. There are no records that he ever took a degree but there is some small evidence that he was being prepared for a career in the church.

However, what is clear is that this was soon abandoned as he joined the stream of people who would leave University and decamp to the more bohemian life of commercial theatre in London.

Unfortunately, his father fell out with Queen Elizabeth but appears to have been on his way to rehabilitation before his death in 1596. At his death he was, however, mired in debt.

The upbringing of the now teenage Fletcher and his seven siblings now passed to his paternal uncle, the poet and minor official Giles Fletcher. Giles, who had the patronage of the Earl of Essex may have been a liability rather than an advantage to the young Fletcher. With Essex involved in the failed rebellion against Elizabeth Giles was also tainted by association.

By 1606 John Fletcher appears to have equipped himself with the talents to become a playwright. Initially this appears to have been for the Children of the Queen's Revels, then performing at the Blackfriars Theatre.

Commendatory verses by Richard Brome in the Beaumont and Fletcher 1647 folio place Fletcher in the company of Ben Jonson, although it is not known when this friendship began. Jonson, of course, was a leviathan of English Literature, so admired that many of his literary friends and colleagues were simply known as 'Sons of Ben'. Fletcher's frequent early collaborator, Francis Beaumont, was also a friend of Jonson's.

Fletcher's early career was marked by one significant failure; The Faithful Shepherdess, his adaptation of Giovanni Battista Guarini's Il Pastor Fido, which was performed by the Blackfriars Children in 1608. In the preface to the printed edition of his play, Fletcher explained the failure as due to his audience's faulty expectations. They expected a pastoral tragicomedy to feature dances, comedy, and murder, with the shepherds presented in conventional stereotypes – as Fletcher put it, wearing "gray cloaks, with curtailed dogs in strings." Fletcher's preface is however best known for its pithy definition of tragicomedy: "A tragicomedy is not so called in respect of mirth and killing, but in respect it wants [i.e., lacks] deaths, which is enough to make it no tragedy; yet brings some near it, which is enough to make it no comedy." A comedy, he went on to say, must be "a representation of familiar people." His preface is critical of drama that features characters whose action violates nature.

In that case, Fletcher appears to have been developing a new style faster than audiences could comprehend. By 1609, however, he had found his stride. With Beaumont, he wrote Philaster, which became a hit for the King's Men and began a profitable association between Fletcher and that company. Philaster appears also to have begun a trend for tragicomedy. Fletcher's influence has also been said to have inspired some features of Shakespeare's late romances, and certainly his influence on the tragicomic work of other playwrights is even more marked.

By the middle of the 1610s, Fletcher's plays had achieved a popularity that rivalled Shakespeare's and cemented the pre-eminence of the King's Men in Jacobean London. After Beaumont's retirement, necessitated by ill-health, and then his early death in 1616, Fletcher continued working, both singly and in collaboration, until his death in 1625. By that time, he had produced, or had been credited with, close to fifty plays. This body of work remained a major part of the King's Men's repertory until the closing of the theatres in 1642 due to the Civil War.

At the beginning of his career Fletcher's most important collaborator was Francis Beaumont. The two wrote together for close to a decade, first for the Children of the Queen's Revels, and then for the King's Men. According to an anecdote transmitted or invented by John Aubrey, they also lived together in Bankside, sharing clothes and having "one wench in the house between them." This domestic arrangement, if it existed, was ended by Beaumont's marriage in 1613, and their dramatic partnership ended after Beaumont fell ill, probably of a stroke, that same year.

At this point Fletcher had written many plays with Beaumont and several others on his own. He seems to have been regarded as quite a talent although it should be remembered that playwrights were required to be prolific, to easily work with other collaborators and to produce work of quality and commercial appeal very quickly.

The King's Men, run by Philip Henslowe, was the most prestigious of the theatre companies and Fletcher now had an increasingly close association with it.

Fletcher collaborated with Shakespeare on Henry VIII, The Two Noble Kinsmen, and the now lost Cardenio, which some scholars say was the basis for Lewis Theobald's play Double Falsehood. (Theobald is regarded as one of the best Shakespearean editors. Whether his play is based on Cardenio or on some other is not absolutely known although Theobald certainly promoted it as his revision of the lost Shakespeare/Fletcher play.)

A play that Fletcher also wrote by himself at this time, The Woman's Prize or the Tamer Tamed, is also regarded as a sequel to The Taming of the Shrew.

In 1616, with the death of Shakespeare, Fletcher now appears to have entered into an enhanced arrangement with the King's Men on very similar terms to Shakespeare's. Fletcher would now write exclusively for the King's Men until his own death almost a decade later.

As well as continuing his solo productions Fletcher was still collaborating with other playwrights, mainly Philip Massinger, who, in turn, would succeed him as the in-house playwright for the King's Men.

Fletcher's popularity continued throughout his life; indeed, during the winter of 1621, he had three of his plays performed at court. His mastery is most notable in two dramatic types; tragicomedy and the comedy of manners.

John Fletcher died in 1625, it is thought of bubonic plague which, at the time, was undergoing further outbreaks.

He seems to have been buried in what is now Southwark Cathedral, although a precise location is not known. There is much made of an anecdote that Fletcher and Massinger (who died in 1640) share the same grave but it is more likely that both are buried within a few yards of each other and that the stone markers in the floor have confused the issue. One is marked 'Edmond Shakespeare 1607' and the other 'John Fletcher 1625' refers to Shakespeare's younger brother and the playwright. The churchyards were, more often than not, completely over-crowded and breeding grounds for disease. Precise record keeping was not a practiced skill.

During the later Commonwealth, many of the playwright's best-known scenes were kept alive as drolls. These were brief performances, usually condensed into one or two scenes and with the addition of music or song to satisfy the taste for plays while the theatres were closed under the Puritans. At the re-opening of the theatres in 1660, the plays in the Fletcher canon, in original form or revised, were by far the most common productions on the English stage. The most frequently revived plays suggest the developing taste for comedies of manners. Among the tragedies, The Maid's Tragedy and, especially, Rollo Duke of Normandy held the stage. Four tragicomedies (A King and No King, The Humorous Lieutenant, Philaster, and The Island Princess) were popular, perhaps in part for their similarity to and foreshadowing of heroic drama. Four comedies (Rule a Wife And Have a Wife, The Chances, Beggars' Bush, and especially The Scornful Lady) were also stage mainstays.

Despite his popularity, and it appears he was held in higher regard than Shakespeare at this time, his works steadily lost ground to those of Shakespeare and to new productions from other playwrights.

Since then Fletcher has increasingly become a subject only for occasional revivals and for specialists. Fletcher and his collaborators have been the subject of important bibliographic and critical studies, but the plays have been revived only infrequently.

Due to the frequent collaborations between all manner of playwrights, and the revisions carried out in later years, having a settled list of authorship to any given set of plays can be problematic. The works of Fletcher and others of this period most definitely fall into this category. It is as well to take into account that during this period theatres were quite often closed either due to outbreaks of the plague or to the prevailing political and moral climate. Printers, anxious to provide materials that would sell, were not above changing a name or two to enhance sales.

Although Fletcher collaborated most often with Beaumont and Massinger, it is believed that Massinger revised many of the plays some time after their original production. Other collaborators including Nathan Field, William Shakespeare, William Rowley and others also can be seen distinctly in Fletchers' works. Many modern scholars point out that Fletcher had many particular mannerisms, but other playwrights would also duplicate these at times so allocating exact contributions of anyone to a play is somewhat of a detective case in many instances. However, from the original folio printings or licensing via the Master of the Revels (the statutory licensing authority to approve and censor plays as well a hand in publication and printing of theatrical materials) as well as contemporary notes a fairly precise bibliography of the works can be given with only a few plays lacking substantial authority and provenance.

This bibliography gives the most likely date of writing together with when published, revised or licensed by the Master or the Revels (This position within the royal household was originally for royal festivities, ie revels, and later to oversee stage censorship, until this function was transferred to the Lord Chamberlain in 1624).

Francis Beaumont – Solo Plays
The Knight of the Burning Pestle, comedy (performed 1607; printed 1613)
The Masque of the Inner Temple and Gray's Inn, masque (printed 1613)

John Fletcher - Solo Plays
The Faithful Shepherdess, pastoral (written 1608–9; printed 1609)
The Tragedy of Valentinian, tragedy (1610–14; 1647)
Monsieur Thomas, comedy (c. 1610–16; 1639)
The Woman's Prize, or The Tamer Tamed, comedy (c. 1611; 1647)
Bonduca, tragedy (1611–14; 1647)
The Chances, comedy (c. 1613–25; 1647)
Wit Without Money, comedy (c. 1614; 1639)
The Mad Lover, tragicomedy (acted 5 January 1617; 1647)
The Loyal Subject, tragicomedy (licensed 16 November 1618; revised 1633; 1647)
The Humorous Lieutenant, tragicomedy (c. 1619; 1647)
Women Pleased, tragicomedy (c. 1619–23; 1647)
The Island Princess, tragicomedy (c. 1620; 1647)
The Wild Goose Chase, comedy (c. 1621; 1652)
The Pilgrim, comedy (c. 1621; 1647)
A Wife for a Month, tragicomedy (licensed 27 May 1624; 1647)
Rule a Wife and Have a Wife, comedy (licensed 19 October 1624; 1640)

Francis Beaumont & John Fletcher
The Woman Hater, comedy (1606; 1607)
Cupid's Revenge, tragedy (c. 1607–12; 1615)
Philaster, or Love Lies a-Bleeding, tragicomedy (c. 1609; 1620)
The Maid's Tragedy, Tragedy (c. 1609; 1619)
A King and No King, tragicomedy (1611; 1619)
The Captain, comedy (c. 1609–12; 1647)
The Scornful Lady, comedy (c. 1613; 1616)
Love's Pilgrimage, tragicomedy (c. 1615–16; 1647)
The Noble Gentleman, comedy (c. 1613; licensed 3 February 1626; 1647)

Their Collaborations with Others

With Philip Massinger
Thierry & Theodoret, tragedy (c. 1607; 1621)
The Coxcomb, comedy (c. 1608–10; 1647)
Beggars' Bush, comedy (c. 1612–13; revised 1622; 1647)
Love's Cure, comedy (c. 1612–13; revised 1625; 1647)

John Fletcher with Philip Massinger
Sir John van Olden Barnavelt, tragedy (August 1619; MS)

The Little French Lawyer, comedy (c. 1619–23; 1647)
A Very Woman, tragicomedy (c. 1619–22; licensed 6 June 1634; 1655)
The Custom of the Country, comedy (c. 1619–23; 1647)
The Double Marriage, tragedy (c. 1619–23; 1647)
The False One, history (c. 1619–23; 1647)
The Prophetess, tragicomedy (licensed 14 May 1622; 1647)
The Sea Voyage, comedy (licensed 22 June 1622; 1647)
The Spanish Curate, comedy (licensed 24 October 1622; 1647)
The Lovers' Progress or The Wandering Lovers, tragicomedy (licensed 6 December 1623; rev 1634; 1647)
The Elder Brother, comedy (c. 1625; 1637)

John Fletcher with Philip Massinger & Nathan Field
The Honest Man's Fortune, tragicomedy (1613; 1647)
The Queen of Corinth, tragicomedy (c. 1616–18; 1647)
The Knight of Malta, tragicomedy (c. 1619; 1647)

John Fletcher with William Shakespeare
Henry VIII, history (c. 1613; 1623)
The Two Noble Kinsmen, tragicomedy (c. 1613; 1634)
Cardenio, tragicomedy (c. 1613)

John Fletcher with Thomas Middleton & William Rowley
Wit at Several Weapons, comedy (c. 1610–20; 1647)

John Fletcher with William Rowley
The Maid in the Mill (licensed 29 August 1623; 1647).

John Fletcher with Nathan Field
Four Plays, or Moral Representations, in One, morality (c. 1608–13; 1647)

John Fletcher with Philip Massinger, Ben Jonson and George Chapman
Rollo Duke of Normandy, or The Bloody Brother, tragedy (c. 1617; revised 1627–30; 1639)

John Fletcher with James Shirley
The Night Walker, or The Little Thief, comedy (c. 1611; 1640)
The Coronation c. 1635

Uncertain
The Nice Valour, or The Passionate Madman, comedy (c. 1615–25; 1647)
The Laws of Candy, tragicomedy (c. 1619–23; 1647)
The Fair Maid of the Inn, comedy (licensed 22 January 1626; 1647)
The Faithful Friends, tragicomedy (registered 29 June 1660; MS.)

The Nice Valour is possibly by Fletcher revised by Thomas Middleton;

The Fair Maid of the Inn is perhaps a play by Massinger, John Ford, and John Webster, either with or without Fletcher's involvement.

The Laws of Candy has been variously attributed to Fletcher and to John Ford.

The Night-Walker was a Fletcher original, with additions by Shirley for a 1639 production.

Even now there is not absolute certainty on several of the plays. The first Beaumont & Fletcher folio of 1647 contained 35 plays and the second folio of 1679 added a further 18. In total 53 plays.

The first folio included The Masque of the Inner Temple and Gray's Inn (1613), and the second The Knight of the Burning Pestle (1607), widely considered Beaumont's solo works, although the latter was in early editions attributed to both writers. Fletcher himself said that Beaumont was attributed co-authorship of many works that belonged solely to Fletcher or to other collaborators.

One play in the canon, Sir John Van Olden Barnavelt, existed in manuscript and was not published till 1883.

www.ingramcontent.com/pod-product-compliance
Lightning Source LLC
Chambersburg PA
CBHW060303050426
42448CB00009B/1733